SHAQUILLE O'NEAL

SHAQUILLE O'NEAL

Ellen Emerson White

SCHOLASTIC INC.
New York Toronto London Auckland Sydney

Photo Credits

Cover photo: © Mitchell Layton/Duomo.
Interior insert: #1 © Tim Defrisco/Allsport; #2 © Bob Daemrich/Allsport; #3 © Jim Gund/Allsport; #4 © John Chiasson/Gamma Liaison; #5 © Tim Defrisco/Allsport; #6 © Ben Van Hook/Duomo; #7 © Jonathan Daniel/Allsport; #8 © John Chiasson/Gamma Liaison.

ISBN 0-590-47785-4

12 11 10 9 8 7   5 6 7 8 9/9

Printed in the U.S.A.   40

First Scholastic printing, January 1994

Acknowledgments

The author would like to thank the following people for their contributions to this biography: Dale Brown, head coach of the Louisiana State University Tigers basketball team; Tim Povtak of the *Orlando Sentinel*; Dave Flores of the *San Antonio Express News*; Scott Dickey of Spalding; Dave Fogelson of Reebok.

Contents

SHAQUILLE O'NEAL

Prologue

It is the rookie's first game on national television, and everyone knows that rookies get nervous. Rookies are inexperienced. Rookies make mistakes.

Even very, very *tall* rookies.

His team, the Orlando Magic, is playing the Phoenix Suns, and basketball fans all over the country have tuned in to watch. The Orlando Magic are an expansion team, still struggling for respect, and not yet ready for greatness. The Suns, led by the fiercely brilliant and always newsworthy Charles Barkley, are one of the best teams in the National Basketball Association. They are a team loaded with talent and veterans. Nothing a rookie can do is going to impress *them*.

The rookie starts off hot, scoring point after point in the first few minutes of the game. But still, the Suns, and the viewers, reserve judgment. Scoring lots of points is something they have seen before.

Then, late in the first quarter, the rookie grabs the ball and slams it through the hoop as hard as he can. He hangs there for a second or two as the backboard shakes all around him. Then, as he drops off the rim, what's left of the backboard, and its entire support system, slowly collapses to the floor.

Even the television commentators are left speechless. Everyone stares at the wreckage on the court. The game is delayed for thirty-five minutes as technicians come out to clear away the mess and set up another backboard. Finally, play continues, but the score is almost forgotten as everyone waits eagerly, hoping to see another amazing Shaq Attaq.

Shaquille O'Neal is not just any rookie.

1
Growing Tall

Shaquille Rashaun O'Neal was born on March 6, 1972, in Newark, New Jersey. The Islamic translation of his name is "little warrior" and — well, he *did* grow up to be a warrior. But he also grew up to be seven feet and one inch tall, and weigh 303 pounds. Even the word "big" doesn't do Shaquille justice.

Shaquille is named for his mother, Lucille O'Neal Harrison, who is over six feet tall herself. Shaquille's father, Phillip A. Harrison, is six feet, five inches tall, and he is a staff sergeant in the Army. Shaquille also has two younger sisters, and a little brother. Lateefah is fifteen, Ayesha is fourteen, and Jamal Hashim is only twelve. They are all very proud of their big brother, and Jamal, who is already almost six feet tall, hopes to follow in Shaquille's footsteps and play basketball.

Since Shaquille wears size 20 sneakers, those will be very big shoes to try to fill.

When he was growing up, Shaquille and his family rarely stayed in one place for very long. Because Shaquille's father is a career soldier, he was often transferred from base to base, and the whole family would come along with him. Over the years, Shaquille has lived on Army bases all over the world, including New Jersey, Georgia, Texas, and West Germany.

Moving around so much can be both exciting and stressful. If a person is at all shy, he or she can find it very difficult to be "the new kid" over and over again, but usually, military children have a special gift for making friends. For one thing, they've had a lot of practice. Also, when a family is as close as Shaquille's family is, leading such an exotic life-style is more enriching than anything else. Today, because of his nomadic childhood, Shaquille finds it very easy to adapt to all sorts of new people, new places, and new situations. This is a very handy skill for a professional athlete to have, since the life of an NBA player involves constant travel, and exposure to different people, particularly fans and reporters.

Shaquille's parents, especially his father, were often very strict, but Shaquille appreciated being brought up with strong values, and a sense of what is right, and what is wrong. This family background, more than anything else, has helped him get where he is today.

4

Sometimes, when he was growing up, Shaquille felt very self-conscious because he was always so much taller than everyone else at each of his schools, and he worried that people would make fun of him. Every time he enrolled at a new school, he would have to face a fresh round of teasing, mostly of the "How's the weather up there?" variety. There were times when he got into fights because of this, but he would usually try to seek out the role of class clown, first. That way, if people were looking at him, he could assume that it was only because they *liked* him.

Then again, Shaquille might also have found himself acting as the class clown because he has such a good sense of humor. Even today, Shaquille describes himself as having one-million, two-million, and *three*-million-dollar smiles. Depending on the situation, he can pull out whichever one seems the most appropriate. The fact that the right side of his mouth tilts up much higher than the left side only makes those lopsided big smiles more charming.

It was obvious early on that Shaquille was going to be very good at sports, but nobody realized that he was going to choose basketball. When his family was living in Jersey City, Shaquille's favorite thing to do was break dance, and he talked about wanting to be a dancer when he grew up. Then, when he was nine years old, Shaquille won first place in all three categories of the

Punt, Pass, and Kick Pee-Wee football competition, and it looked as though football might be the activity that he was going to choose.

The first time Shaquille's father saw his son pick up a basketball, he had a feeling that he was going to be something special. But as far as Shaquille was concerned, basketball was just another fun thing to do, and not a game to take that seriously.

When Shaquille was ten, Sergeant Harrison was transferred to an Army post in Wildflecken, Germany, where American troops were stationed along the East German border to help maintain the peace that seemed so fragile before the Berlin Wall came down some years later. While his family was living there, Shaquille spent more time fooling around with his friends than he did getting good grades, but when he was thirteen, something happened that changed his life.

Dale Brown, the celebrated head coach from Louisiana State University, was traveling around West Germany, giving motivational speeches to military troops on the various bases spread across the country. What happened at the last base he visited would change *his* life, too.

Coach Brown remembers his first meeting with Shaquille this way. "My last speech, after weeks in Germany, was right on the East German border, at a place called Wildflecken, up in the mountains," he said, in an interview. "I finished up my speech that night, and I was packing my bags, and I got a tap on the shoulder. I turned around, and there was this man standing there."

"Coach Brown, I wonder if I can get some help from you," the young man said tentatively.

"Certainly," Coach Brown answered.

"I'm very, very upset with my lower extremities," the young man said. "I don't have a real good vertical jump and I fatigue easily. I wonder if you could give me some exercises to do—weights, or whatever."

Coach Brown was often asked for this sort of advice, and his response was automatic. "What I'll do first," Coach Brown said, "is I'll show you some exercises you can use *without* weights, and then I'll get your name and address, and I'll send you our weight program."

The young man nodded eagerly.

After demonstrating the exercises, Coach Brown turned to get the young man's name and address. "How long have you been in the service, soldier?" he asked, out of curiosity.

The young man looked startled, then leaned forward. "*I'm* not in the service," he whispered.

Coach Brown stared at him. "You're *not*?"

The young man shook his head. "No. I'm only thirteen years old."

The young "soldier" was, of course, Shaquille.

"Thirteen years old?!" Coach Brown said, unable to believe that this 6'8" person standing in front of him could actually be in *junior high*. "What size shoe do you have?"

"Seventeen," Shaquille answered.

"Well — " Coach Brown was still having trouble taking this in. "What are you doing here?"

"My father's in the Army," Shaquille told him. "He's a career military man, and we've been stationed here."

"Well," Coach Brown said. "I'd like to meet your father!"

Shaquille explained that his father was in the sauna, and he and Coach Brown walked over there. Sergeant Harrison was just coming out, and Coach Brown introduced himself, then handed the sergeant his card.

"If your son ever develops into a player — " Coach Brown started.

Shaquille's father shook his head, cutting him off. "Coach, I'm not concerned about basketball, I'm concerned about blacks developing intellectually, so they can be presidents of corporations, *head* coaches instead of assistants, and *generals* in the Army instead of sergeants like me. If my son ever develops, and you're interested in his intellect, too — fine."

Five years later, Shaquille was a freshman at LSU, and just happened to have the highest grade point average on the *team*.

As it turned out, not *every* coach was as observant when it came to noticing Shaquille's potential as a basketball player.

"The next year," Coach Brown said, talking about when Shaquille was fourteen, "when he tried out for basketball at the base in Fulda, West

Germany, he was cut from the team, and the coach told him, 'You should be a goalie in soccer. You're too slow, you've got too big feet, and you're too clumsy.' "

Today, wherever he is now, that coach must feel pretty embarrassed.

2
State Champions

In 1987, during the spring of Shaquille's sophomore year, Sergeant Harrison was posted to Fort
Sam Houston in San Antonio, Texas. The family
moved back to the United States, and Shaquille
enrolled in Robert G. Cole High School. Having
grown out of his junior high mischievousness,
Shaquille started paying attention in class, and
received much better grades. His parents were
very pleased.

That fall, Shaquille joined the Cole High School
basketball team, and led them to the Texas State
Class 2A Regional Finals, scoring 522 points during the season. Cole lost to a school named Liberty Hill, by a score of 79–74, and the team's final
record that year was 32 victories, with just that
one defeat.

The following year, Shaquille and his teammates were determined to avenge the loss to Liberty Hill, and go all the way to the state championship. By now, Shaquille's combination of height and talent had gained the attention of the media, and coaches from colleges all over the country were already trying to recruit him. He became the most eagerly pursued high school player in the nation, and since he was only sixteen, it would have been very easy to let all of that praise and attention go to his head. But Shaquille's parents were careful to make sure that their son always behaved politely, and kept up with his schoolwork. Sergeant and Mrs. Harrison both firmly believed that Shaquille's education was far more important than his skills on the basketball court, and so Shaquille was able to keep things in perspective.

In Shaquille's senior year, he scored an average of 32.1 points per game, also averaging 22 rebounds and eight blocked shots. During the 36 games that Cole High School played, Shaquille scored a total of 1,123 points — many of them on thunderous, backboard-shaking dunks. It was obvious that he was a player with a very *big* future.

Shaquille's team went back to the Class 3A Regional Finals (having moved up a division during the off-season realignment), where they — once again — met their archrival, Liberty Hill. The Texas high school state tournament is held every year at the University of Texas in Austin, and everyone there was watching the team from Cole

High School with the smiling young center who was almost seven feet tall.

Cole beat Liberty Hill in the Regional Finals, 85–72. Their next opponent, in the semifinals, was Hearne High School, and Shaquille and his teammates won easily, 69–56. Now they were just one game away from the Texas Class 3A State Championship. They faced Clarksville High in the finals. It was an exciting game, but Shaquille and his teammates pulled out a solid 66–60 win, giving them an undefeated season — and the championship.

It was a happy trip back to San Antonio.

Over the two years of Shaquille's high school career, his team won 68 games and lost only one. Shaquille was selected to every All-Star team for which he was eligible, including the All-Greater San Antonio team and the Class 3A All-Star All-State team. He was also designated the Player of the Year in Greater San Antonio.

"His senior year, you could tell that he was going to be special," Dave Flores, a reporter for *San Antonio Express News*, who covered Shaquille in high school, said in a recent interview. "It was really amazing to see somebody that age have not only the skills, but also the physical attributes, and the *style*. When I saw him, he never looked awkward at all."

In the wake of Cole High School's 36–0 season, Shaquille continued to receive accolades every time he turned around. He was chosen the Most Valuable Player of two national invitation-only games, the McDonald's All-Star Classic, and the Dapper Dan Classic. Even more impressively, *Parade* magazine chose him as the center on their All-America team.

"Keep in mind, his birthday is on March 6th, so he had only just turned seventeen when he graduated from high school," reporter Dave Flores said. "Certainly, there have been big men with finesse, but I don't think there's ever been that big a guy, with that kind of frame, who carried his weight, and height, so well. We always referred to him as a man-child."

Whether he was a man or a child, Shaquille was definitely the focus of national attention now, as sports reporters wrote flattering stories, and college coaches called him constantly, hoping that he would sign a letter of intent with their respective basketball programs. But, over the years, Coach Brown from LSU had always kept in touch and, knowing that he was genuinely concerned about Shaquille's welfare — and education — Shaquille and his parents decided that he would attend Louisiana State University in the fall.

Shaquille was about to go from being one of the most famous high school players in the country to being one of the most famous college players.

*   *   *

It is probably a good idea to pause here, and talk a little about the sport of basketball. Everyone knows that there are two teams, with five players on each side, who all run up and down the court trying to throw a big orange ball into a hoop. But the game is much more complicated than that.

There are five positions on a basketball team, and each one serves a different function. The point guard is usually the smallest member of the team, who makes up for his or her lack of height by being quick and alert. During the game, the point guard will bring the ball down the court, and run all the plays from the top of the key. A good point guard will rack up lots of assists— which are awarded when a player passes the ball to another player, who then scores — but most point guards are so busy keeping everyone else involved in the flow of the game that they don't get many opportunities to shoot the ball themselves. John Stockton of the Utah Jazz and Mark Price of the Cleveland Cavaliers are classic examples of ideal point guards.

Next comes the shooting (or off-guard) guard, who generally plays in the backcourt with the point guard. The shooting guard is almost as good a ball handler as the point guard, and sometimes, depending on the game situation, they will trade responsibilities. Shooting guards also tend to be smaller than average players, and rely on agility and hustle. On both offense and defense, the guards stay in the backcourt, and so end up doing almost no rebounding. Mainly, the shooting guard's job is to shoot deadly accurate jump shots and three-pointers, and give his or her team an outside scoring threat. Clyde Drexler of the Portland Trail Blazers and Joe Dumars of the Detroit Pistons fall into this category.

It is worth mentioning that although Michael Jordan, technically speaking, plays guard, he is so much better than everyone else on the face of the planet that he is impossible to categorize.

Then, there are two forwards — a small (or shooting, or point) forward, and a power forward. The descriptions of their jobs are fairly self-explanatory, but the best way to describe the two positions is to say that the small forward is often a team's leading scorer, and the power forward is likely to be the top rebounder. A truly great player, like Charles Barkley, will do both jobs, but ordinarily, one forward is a shooter, while the other is a rebounder. Charles Oakley from the New York Knicks and Pistons player Dennis Rodman are good examples of frontcourt power forwards, while Dominique Wilkins of the Atlanta Hawks and Larry Johnson of the Charlotte Hornets match the description of shooting forwards.

Finally, every team is built around their center. The center (who used to be known as the pivot player, since she or he would not move, so much as pivot in place under the basket) is the biggest, and almost always the most dominating, player on the team. Most offensive plays are geared around getting the ball in to the center, who will then take the easy shot. While on defense, the center is the player on whom the final responsibility of protecting the basket falls. A team with a great center can get away with making a lot of other mistakes, since the center will be the major factor in the game, anyway.

Most people would agree that the three best centers in the NBA are Patrick Ewing from the New York Knicks, David Robinson, who plays for the San Antonio Spurs, and Hakeem Olajuwon, the center for the Houston Rockets. All three men are 7'0", or 7'1", but beyond just being tall, they are multidimensional athletes. After all, if just being tall was enough to make a player a star, Manute Bol, at 7'7", would be the best player in history. Great centers will usually lead their teams in scoring, rebounding, blocked shots, and inspiration. Having the right "big man" may not be enough to guarantee a championship, but *without* an elite center, a team won't even come close.

Shaquille, of course, is a center. What may, ultimately, make him even greater than the three players discussed above, is the athleticism that goes along with his size. Shaquille has very little body fat — somewhere between 7.5 and 10 percent — and is extremely mobile for a seven-footer. He is also faster than he has any right to be, and can even be seen dribbling the ball up-court sometimes. The combination of Shaquille's strength, speed, and versatility make him a bundle of raw skills who may one day change the definition of a center the same way Michael Jordan redefined the notion of what a guard can be.

Historically, some of the best, and most memorable, players in the game have been centers. True fans can spend happy hours debating about who was, or is, the best center ever. The three names people mention most often are Wilt Chamberlain, Bill Russell, and Kareem Abdul-Jabbar.

Wilt Chamberlain played for fourteen years, and set more records than even a person with a photographic memory could recite. He won the league's Most Valuable Player award four times, and was chosen to play in thirteen All-Star games. He averaged over 30 points per game during his career, led the league in scoring seven years in a row, and holds the all-time record for points scored in a game. He set that record against the Knicks in 1962, scoring exactly 100 points. No one else has come close to that figure, before or since. His average of 50.4 points-per-game during the 1961–62 season is also the highest in basketball history. Wilt holds the records for the most rebounds in a season — 2,149 — and the most career rebounds, with a whopping total of 23,924. He also helped his team win world championships in both Los Angeles and Philadelphia.

Bill Russell is another worthy candidate for the best center in the history of the NBA. During his thirteen years with the Celtics, Boston won *eleven* world championships — a record comparable only to the New York Yankees baseball dynasties. Bill was the Most Valuable Player five times, and played in eleven All-Star games. Maybe the most important aspect of Bill's career was that he was the first black athlete to become a superstar in the NBA. In the early years of professional basketball, racism was as much a problem as it was throughout the rest of American society, and Bill bore the brunt of other people's bigotry and hostility, never once losing his own integrity and dignity. Before Bill Russell came along, the concept of five black athletes playing on the floor at the same time — forget holding an overwhelming majority of the playing positions in the NBA— would have seemed inconceivable. Later, when he served as a player-coach for Boston, he widened the opportunities available for a person of color even more.

Kareem Abdul-Jabbar is the other most common choice as the best center in NBA history. Kareem played for twenty years, and holds the all-time scoring record with 38,387 points, as well as having the all-time record in at least seven other categories. After being chosen as the Rookie of the Year his first season, Kareem played in eighteen All-Star games, and was the league's MVP on six different occasions. Kareem also played on six world championship squads.

Shaquille's favorite player when he was growing up was Hall of Famer Julius "Dr. J." Erving, but he also admired all of the great centers. Today, many people think that Shaquille will not only be as good as those great stars, but may even one day surpass them.

For now, that is still a dream of Shaquille's, but it is one that he just might achieve someday.

3
The First Big Step

The Louisiana State Tigers have traditionally been a basketball power, but when Shaquille joined the team as a freshman, a number of magazines and newspapers picked the team to finish first in the country. For example, *Sport Magazine* ranked LSU number one in its pre-season college basketball issue, followed by perennial choice Michigan, the always fiercely competitive UNLV (University of Nevada, Las Vegas), southwest powerhouse Arizona, and in the fifth position, Georgetown, whose team included one of the other top college centers in the country, Alonzo Mourning. The other teams in the top ten were Syracuse, North Carolina, Duke, Arkansas, and Clemson.

But Shaquille wasn't the only great player on the Tigers. Chris Jackson was considered the top point guard in the nation, and hulking Stanley Roberts was a superb center, who gave the 1989–90 Tigers potential "Twin Tower" power. The expression "Twin Towers" refers to when a team uses *two* center-type players simultaneously, allowing them to completely control the game from a height perspective, although they may give up a lot in speed and versatility.

Dennis Tracey was considered the Tigers' best defensive player, while Wayne Sims was an excellent shooter. Other members of the team included Geert Hammink, Vernel Singleton, and Randy Devall. Harold Boudreaux, a potentially great young player, had "redshirted," in order to spend his freshman year concentrating on his studies. When players redshirt, they sit out a full season, without damaging their eligibility for future seasons. As it happened, Harold's redshirting was a good idea, because he ended up on the Dean's List.

In its preview issue, *Sport Magazine* had also picked Shaquille as the number three center in the country, and Chris Jackson as the number one point guard. The Tigers were loaded with talent, and everyone was looking forward to the new season.

The Tigers play all of their home games in the Pete Maravich Assembly Center, which was named for the late, great former NBA star. Maravich Assembly Center has a 13,479-person capacity, and when the Tigers are playing, every single one of those seats is filled. In fact, LSU fans

22

are so loyal and noisy that the nickname for the Center is "the Deaf Zone."

Coach Brown had become known, over the years, for trying all sorts of new things on the basketball court, including what he calls the "freak defense." But with so many good players on the team, he wasn't going to need any fancy tricks to steal ballgames, and he planned to use more traditional offensive and defensive schemes, like the 1–2–2 zone. Mainly, he wanted his team to take advantage of their speed — since most teams were slowed down by having big, clumsy centers, and Shaquille was anything but that — and play a very up-tempo game. Or, as Coach Brown often put it, he wanted his team to run, run, *run*.

As a freshman, Shaquille was a combination of size and raw talent. He had a great attitude, and astonishing agility for a seven-footer. The two main things he needed to work on were his free-throw shooting, which was atrocious, and developing some sort of outside shot, be it a hook or a jumper.

Off the court, Shaquille was enjoying school, and planning to major in business administration. He was carrying a 3.0 grade point average, which works out to a solid B average. Considering how much time he had to spend practicing with the team, and traveling to games, this was a remarkable achievement.

"He was a model citizen at LSU," Coach Brown says now. "No drugs, no alcohol, and he always went to class. He had the highest grade point average on our whole team that year — and well, the rest is history."

The Tigers had a somewhat disappointing season, posting a 23–9 record. Coach Brown found that the youth and inexperience of his team was its biggest problem, and sometimes he had trouble motivating them to run as much as he wanted. Because of this, the Tigers' play was somewhat inconsistent.

Shaquille's play reflected this inconsistency. For example, in a game against Duke University and their marquee star Christian Laettner, Shaquille only scored five points and grabbed 10 rebounds. Christian came up with 11 rebounds, and 24 points, and Duke won easily, 88–70. But then, against Loyola Marymount, Shaquille set two SEC (Southeastern Conference) records with 24 rebounds and 12 blocked shots.

In the SEC tournament, the Tigers lost to Auburn University, and Shaquille only scored 10 points, with eight rebounds. But, that loss didn't keep LSU from being invited to the NCAA tournament, the winner of which is declared the top college team in the country.

However, the Tigers lost early in the tournament to Georgia Tech, despite Shaquille's 19 points and 14 rebounds. But Georgia Tech point guard Kenny Anderson, who now stars for the NBA's New Jersey Nets, and the other Georgia Tech Yellow Jackets were too good for LSU, and the Tigers' season was over.

Shaquille finished his freshman year with an average of 13.9 points, 12.0 rebounds, and six blocked shots per game. In 32 games, he had 21 "double-doubles" (when a player reaches double figures in both points and rebounds) and two *triple*-doubles, where in addition to scoring and rebounding in double figures, a player also has at least ten blocked shots. Shaquille also led the SEC with 385 rebounds and 115 blocked shots.

On the whole, Shaquille was very pleased with his first season, although he knew he needed to work on committing fewer fouls, since he had fouled out of *nine* games, which was almost a third of the games the team had played.

Now, he was looking forward to his summer vacation. He had a job with a construction company in Louisiana, and enjoyed the hard work and physical activity. Every day, when he wasn't working, Shaquille played basketball, and at night, he would do exercises like calf raises in his room, always trying to improve his jumping ability. The exercises paid off, because in the fall, he was able to jump a full *eight* inches higher than he had the year before.

Shaquille was invited to play in a number of summer tournaments, but turned down prestigious events like the World Games and the Goodwill Games so that he could have fun on his vacation. However, when an invitation came from the Olympic Festival, a tournament held in Minneapolis, Coach Brown encouraged Shaquille to go. The Festival showcases Olympic hopefuls (this was before the Olympic basketball team was composed almost entirely of NBA stars), and Shaquille stole the show.

In four games, he set a Festival record by scoring 98 points and grabbing 58 rebounds, an accomplishment to which he added 27 blocked shots. The previous record had stood at 77 points and 57 rebounds over the four-game series. Shaquille starred for the South team, which beat the North team in the gold medal finals. The North team included such future NBA stars as Tim Hardaway.

In that final game, Shaquille scored a Festival-record 39 points, but the spectators were more thrilled when he tore the rim right off the backboard while dunking.

Most of them had never seen Shaquille play before, but now, they couldn't wait to see him again.

In the fall, Shaquille returned to LSU for his sophomore season. This year, *Sport Magazine* was only picking the Tigers to finish seventh in the nation, since they had lost some of their best players from the season before. Point guard Chris Jackson had left college early and gone into the NBA draft, where he was selected by the Denver Nuggets. Burly big man Stanley Roberts had run into academic problems and dropped out, going over to Spain to play professional basketball in the European league. Dennis Tracey had suffered a bad knee injury, and Maurice Williamson and

Randy Devall were both academically ineligible.

The Tigers had some new players, including transfer student Mike Hansen, who became Shaquille's close friend and co-captain, but Shaquille knew he had to step up and deliver a monster season if the Tigers were to accomplish anything.

Shaquille started his season off with a bang while playing an exhibition game against an Australian team, the Newcastle Falcons. While hanging onto the rim after a slam-dunk, he broke the chain that held the backboard support system in place and nearly pulled the whole thing over. Privately, that was one of his goals, and he came close to it several times during the season, but didn't manage that feat until after he joined the NBA.

A couple of weeks later, while playing Villanova in the Hall of Fame game in Springfield, Massachusetts, Shaquille went up for a jam, and moved the backboard supports about half a foot to one side. One day soon, especially if he played on a court without breakaway rims, he knew he would knock an entire backboard down.

Wanting to help his young center progress even faster as a player, Coach Brown invited several former NBA stars to come down to LSU and work with Shaquille intensively. That group included players like Bill Walton, Kareem Abdul-Jabbar, and Julius "Dr. J." Erving. Shaquille was very excited by the opportunity to meet some of his idols, and happy to take any advice they offered.

In a nationally televised game against the

number-two college team in the country, the Arizona Wildcats, Shaquille and his teammates surprised everyone by winning, 92–82. Shaquille scored 29 points, to go along with 14 rebounds and six blocked shots, while Kareem Abdul-Jabbar watched admiringly from the stands. When Shaquille came swooping in for the slam-dunk that clinched the victory, he went into an impromptu dance, captured for posterity by the television cameras.

When asked by reporters after the game what he had been doing, Shaquille explained gravely that it was the Shaq-de-Shaq. He also reminded them that Shaq should always be spelled with a "q," and never with a boring "ck." Shaquille had spent so much time being interviewed that he had learned to enjoy the process, and liked to use what he called "SHAM" when he responded to their questions. "SHAM," as it turned out, stood for "Short-Answer Method."

Years before officially becoming a pro, Shaquille was *already* a pro.

4
Unreal Shaquille

Later that December, Shaquille scored 53 points — his personal high while in college— against Arkansas State, giving the basketball world yet another indication that he was a player to watch.

The Tigers continued their winning ways, beating teams like Auburn, Vanderbilt, Georgia, and Rick Pitino's powerful Kentucky squad. In these games, Shaquille generally scored about 30 points, pulled down 15 rebounds, and blocked five shots. For almost every other college player, those "averages" would be more like personal bests.

Shaquille and his teammates played somewhat less well on the road, losing to teams like Villanova, Illinois, and Duke University. One of the reasons for this was that Shaquille inevitably ran into foul trouble in these road games, and either fouled out of the game, or ended up spending too much time on the bench.

Then, in a game against Florida in late February, Shaquille broke his left leg. It was only a hairline fracture, just below his knee, but that didn't make it hurt any less. Reeling without their great center, the Tigers lost their final game of the regular season against Mississippi State by a low 76–73 score. That gave LSU a final record of 20 wins and 10 losses, which was good enough to make them co-champions of the Southeastern Conference.

From there, the Tigers went to the SEC Championship and lost to Auburn in the first round. If anyone had doubted Shaquille's importance to the team before, they no longer did, as the Tigers were ousted from the tournament.

Even though it had been just over two weeks since Shaquille had suffered his broken leg, he decided to come back and play against the Connecticut Huskies in the first round of the NCAA tournament. He was a little out of shape from his unexpected layoff, but ready to give it his best effort.

LSU was seeded sixth in the tournament, and Connecticut was the eleventh seed, so most observers assumed that the Tigers would win easily. Shaquille played hard, ignoring the pain in his leg, and scored 27 points, nine of his eleven field goals coming on dunks. He also had 16 rebounds and five blocked shots. But no one else on the team scored more than seven points, and after leading early in the game, LSU faltered and the Huskies took over.

The Tigers shot only 32 percent from the field, so the Huskies were able to concentrate their defensive efforts on Shaquille, seeing that no one else was going to pick up the slack. Led by Chris Smith's 25 points and John Gwynn's 17, Connecticut was winning by 11 points at halftime, and finished with a 79–62 shocker of a victory, eliminating the Tigers from the tournament.

It was discouraging not to have gone further in the NCAAs, but other than that, Shaquille's season had been stupendous. He was a unanimous first team, All-America selection, joining future NBA players Larry Johnson, Billy Owens, Stacey Augmon, and Kenny Anderson.

Shaquille was the first player ever to lead the SEC in scoring, field goal percentage, rebounds, *and* blocked shots — all in the same season. He averaged 27.6 points, 14.7 rebounds, and 5.0 blocked shots per game. The 5.0 blocked shots average set a national record for college sophomores. For the second year in a row, Shaquille led the SEC in rebounding, and that 14.7 average also led the entire nation.

To go along with his All-America honors, Shaquille was unanimously chosen SEC Player of the Year, and designated the MVP of the SEC All-Defensive team. He was also given National Player of the Year awards by United Press International, the Associated Press, *Sports Illustrated*, and L.A. Gear, and won the Tanqueray World Amateur Athlete of the Year award as well.

All in all, Shaquille's sophomore season had been quite a success.

For no particular reason, Shaquille started off his junior year in a slump. The Tigers lost badly to teams like Arizona and UNLV, and it looked like it was going to be a terrible season. But, after receiving tough pep talks from just about everyone he knew — including his grandmother — Shaquille started playing better and was soon back to his normal, overwhelming self. His grades also came back up close to Dean's List status, after a sophomore dip down to a 2.0 grade point average.

The Tigers went on a winning streak, with nine victories in a row, including two over highly ranked Alabama and Kentucky, giving them a 13–4 win-loss record halfway through the season. The team did well against many of the weaker teams on their schedule, like Nicholls State, Southeastern Louisiana, Northern Arizona, and McNeese State, but Shaquille was getting tired of teams guarding him with as many as *four* other players in an attempt to shut down his production. The other teams' dramatic tactics didn't really work, but Shaquille was getting banged around so much that basketball seemed like less fun than usual.

Against Duke University, the team that later won the NCAA tournament, the Tigers came close to winning, and Shaquille played better against Duke star Christian Laettner than he ever had before, with 25 points and 12 rebounds, compared to Christian's 22 points and 10 rebounds. For some reason, Shaquille had always had trouble when he played against Christian. It would have been nice if his successful effort this time had been enough to give the Tigers a victory, but Duke won by 10 points, largely because LSU missed 10 out of 13 foul shots in the last six minutes of the game. Shaquille was very upset about this since four of those missed shots had been his.

The Tigers ended the year with a 21 and 10 record, moving on to the SEC tournament. Everything was going fine until they met Tennessee in the quarterfinals. With ten minutes left to play and LSU holding a comfortable lead, one of the Tennessee players, Carlius Groves, grabbed Shaquille from behind while he was going up for a dunk, and a fight broke out that lasted almost half an hour. The benches cleared, and when the referees finally got the situation under control, ten players were ejected. To make matters worse, Shaquille was given a one-game suspension — for the SEC Conference Championship game — and Coach Brown got an official reprimand. In all the excitement, people barely noticed that LSU had won the game, 99–89.

Coach Brown was furious about what had happened, since he felt that Groves's actions had been completely unnecessary, and not only did he threaten to have his team boycott the finals, but he also recommended that Shaquille give up his final year of eligibility and enter the 1992 NBA draft. In Coach Brown's opinion, Shaquille was risking physical injury by staying in college ball, where players who couldn't guard him were reduced to grabbing him or knocking him down.

The Tigers met Kentucky in the Conference Championship game, but without Shaquille, they really didn't have a chance, especially when every member of Kentucky's starting five scored in double figures. Harold Boudreaux, who took over for Shaquille at center, was able to score only five points, with two rebounds, and in spite of senior Justin Anderson's 21 points, the Tigers went down in defeat.

LSU was invited to the NCAA tournament, and since his suspension had only lasted for one game, Shaquille was able to play. In the first round, against Brigham Young's Cougars, Shaquille set a tournament record by blocking a colossal 11 of Brigham Young's shot attempts. He also scored 26 points, with 13 rebounds.

In the fourth quarter, the Cougars were behind by only five points, but LSU reversed their foul-shooting problems of the past by knocking down 11 out of 12 in the waning moments of the game. The final score was LSU, 94, and Brigham Young, 83, so the Tigers moved on to the second round.

People were so busy looking ahead to the probable LSU/Georgetown match-up in an upcoming round that they forgot that LSU might not get past Indiana, their second-round opponent. Since Alonzo Mourning, the other best college center in the country, played for Georgetown, and he and Shaquille had never played against each other before, the thought of such a duel was very enticing.

As it developed, Indiana had something else in mind, knocking LSU out of the tournament by an 89–79 score. Shaquille scored 36 points, but Indiana's Calbert Cheaney had 30, with his teammate Allan Henderson adding 19. Once again, the Tigers had gotten nowhere near the Final Four in the NCAA tournament.

For the second year in a row, Shaquille was a consensus pick for the All-America team, and was chosen the SEC Player of the Year. He was L.A. Gear's National Player of the Year for the second time, and was the runner-up for the Naismith and John Wooden Awards, given to the top college player. (Christian Laettner won both awards.)

Shaquille was the first player since Charles Barkley to lead the SEC in rebounding for three years in a row, and he had also set an SEC record for the most blocks in a season for the third time. His 14.0 rebounding average topped the nation, and he led the SEC in field goal percentage, and blocked shots, while coming in second in scoring. He also had had three more triple-double games, and had scored in double figures for the last 63 games in a row. Finally, he was the first LSU player to have more than 400 rebounds two years running, and the third LSU player to score more than 700 points twice.

But now that Shaquille's junior year was over, it was time to think seriously about whether he would stay in school, or turn pro. Shaquille was torn, since if he stayed in school he would be the first person on either side of his family ever to graduate from college, and his parents were *strongly* encouraging him to finish.

In the end though, after consulting with Coach Brown, and his new agent, Leonard Armato, Shaquille decided that he would leave school. He announced this at a press conference back at Fort Sam, surrounded by his family. He explained that he would keep working on his business administration degree during the off-seasons, but that he was no longer enjoying playing at the college level and would now be entering the NBA draft.

It was time to move on.

5
Shaquille Makes a Deal

Basketball is a fun game to watch and play, but professional basketball is also a business. When a player like Shaquille is available in the college draft, basketball becomes very *big* business.

Each year, before the basketball draft, a lottery is held, using Ping-Pong balls, in order to decide which team will get to make the first pick. Obviously, every team wants the opportunity to choose the best player available, but in order to make the selection process fair, teams with poorer win-loss records are given more opportunities to win in the lottery.

Once a team is given the right to make the first pick, the business aspects of basketball kick in. Unlike most other professional sports, the NBA has set up a salary cap for each team, so that salaries won't go out of control, the way they have in baseball, and so that teams in cities that sell fewer tickets and receive less media attention will be able to compete on an equal basis.

When the 1992 draft lottery was held on May 17, the Orlando Magic, one of the new expansion teams, won and were given the first pick of the draft. Since Shaquille was the best player to have come along in years, everyone knew that the Magic wanted to select him, but there were rumors going around that Shaquille only wanted to play in Los Angeles, for either the Clippers or the Lakers, and that he would refuse to sign a contract. Still other rumors suggested that he might go play in Europe, and pass up the NBA altogether.

The Orlando Magic were going to have to work hard to get Shaquille to join their team. The first pick in the 1991 draft, Larry Johnson, had cost the Charlotte Hornets almost twenty million dollars for a six-year contract, but as the best player to come into the league since Patrick Ewing — and potentially the best player ever — Shaquille's contract was going to cost much more.

If Shaquille decided not to play for Orlando, he had several different options. He could make it clear that he would not sign a contract for *any* amount of money, and Orlando might trade their rights to the number-one pick to another team. Shaquille could decide not to play at all for a year, and just finish up his degree at Louisiana State University, and then he could go back into the draft in 1993. If he decided not to play at all for *two* years, then he would be an unrestricted free agent, which would mean that he could sign a contract with any of the teams in the NBA, and just skip the draft entirely. But that would also mean that Shaquille wouldn't be able to play the game that he loved, unless he left the United States and joined a team overseas.

The main reason Shaquille wanted to play in Los Angeles is because Los Angeles is a big city, filled with excitement and celebrities, and a place where it would be very easy for him to become a star. While Orlando has Disney World and Sea World, it is not nearly as cosmopolitan, and very far away from the bright lights of Hollywood. The Orlando Magic were also handicapped by the fact that the team had only existed for three years, and had never come close to making the playoffs before. Playing for a team that couldn't compete with the best of the NBA wouldn't be much fun. On the other hand, Shaquille is such a great player that he could probably make *any* team good enough to play competitively with teams like the Chicago Bulls and the New York Knicks.

On June 24, the Orlando Magic decided to take a chance, and selected Shaquille with the first pick in the draft. Somehow, they would figure out a way to sign him. While Shaquille was the obvious first choice, the next few picks in the draft were fairly predictable, too. Alonzo Mourning, the Georgetown center who had so often been compared to Shaquille, was chosen by the Charlotte Hornets with the number-two pick. Christian Laettner, the forward from Duke who had beaten Shaquille out for both the Naismith and John Wooden Player of the Year awards, was taken by the Minnesota Timberwolves with the third pick. Next, Jimmy Jackson, from Ohio State, went to the Dallas Mavericks, and the fifth pick was LaPhonso Ellis from Notre Dame, who would now be playing for the Denver Nuggets.

In the end, of course, Shaquille decided that he would like to play for Orlando, and the front office management for the Magic, and Shaquille's agent, Leonard Armato, just had to figure out how to make a Shaquille Deal.

The first problem that came up was when Shaquille's old teammate from LSU, Stanley Roberts, who played for the Orlando Magic now, was offered a five-year contract offer sheet from the Dallas Mavericks worth almost fifteen million dollars. Roberts was a good player and the Magic didn't want to lose him, but it was going to be hard to sign him, *and* sign Shaquille at the same time, while staying within the NBA's fourteen-million-dollar salary cap.

The rules for signing players are very complicated, but the most important part to remember is that a team can go slightly over its salary cap to sign a player who is *already* on the team, but not to sign a new player. So, Orlando was going to have to sign Shaquille first, and then try to make a deal with Stanley Roberts.

It was going to cost at least three million dollars to sign Shaquille for the first year, and Orlando only had about one million dollars available. Somehow, they had to come up with the rest.

So, they went to some of the other players on the team, and asked if they would be willing to accept big cuts in their own salaries in order to sign this great new rookie. Four players — Greg Kite, Terry Catledge, Scott Skiles, and Jerry Reynolds — all agreed to do so, and the cuts in their salaries added up to almost half of the two million dollars the Magic needed. Then, the Magic traded Sam Vincent, who was making a very high salary, to the Milwaukee Bucks, for Lester Conner, who was making a much lower salary. Lester also agreed to have his salary cut an extra hundred thousand dollars, for a total savings of seven hundred thousand dollars. Finally, one other player who refused to take a salary cut was released, and the Magic had the two million dollars they needed to sign Shaquille.

The funny part was that after all that trouble, Orlando ended up trading Stanley Roberts to the Los Angeles Clippers, anyway.

So now, Shaquille was a full-fledged member of the Orlando Magic, posing for pictures in their black-and-blue-pinstriped uniform, and the hype was building every day. The contract he finally signed was estimated to be worth forty million dollars, spread out over seven years, which, at the time, was the biggest contract ever signed by an athlete. (Barry Bonds of the San Francisco Giants, among others, has now passed that figure.)

Shaquille's new teammates wanted to have a winning team, so they had been happy to renegotiate their contracts to help sign him, but now, Shaquille needed to do something to return their generosity. All his teammates wanted was for him to play well, but Shaquille still decided to do something to make it obvious that he didn't think he was more important than the rest of the team. He had worn the number 33 both in high school and college, but on the Orlando Magic, that number already belonged to Terry Catledge, a seven-year veteran forward. Shaquille immediately volunteered to give up his lucky number, and wear the number 32 instead. It was a small gesture, but one that pleased his new team very much. As Magic Johnson and many other great players have shown, with their reliance on passing the ball and keeping everyone else on the court involved with the flow of the game, a generous athlete is much better than a selfish one.

After all, basketball is a *team* sport.

Shaquille spent the rest of the summer getting ready for his first year as a professional basketball player. It was generally assumed that he would thrive in the competitive environment of the NBA, but he would be facing a number of adjustments in going from the college level to the pro game. For one thing, he would be facing a whole new array of pressure defenses, since college teams usually play in zones, like the box-and-one. Also, of course, he would be playing against top players every single night, instead of running into the fluctuating skills levels found at different college programs in any given year. In the NBA, *everyone* is a top-flight player.

While Shaquille joined in various pickup games organized by other pro players, he also participated in two more organized events. First, he was pleased to be asked to play in Magic Johnson's Annual All-Star Game, where star players came together to earn money for the United Negro College Fund. Shaquille had a great time, scoring 36 points, to go along with 19 rebounds. This was the first opportunity for some of the other stars to play against Shaquille, and they were all almost more impressed by his maturity than they were by his prodigious skills.

Also in August, Shaquille attended Pete Newell's famous Big Man Camp. Pete, who is seventy-seven, has run the clinic for many years, and only the *literal*, as well as figurative, giants of the game are invited to come. The camp is a series of comprehensive work sessions, so that centers (and maybe the odd power forward here and there) can concentrate on refining the very specific skills their position requires. Many "big men" need help learning how to take advantage of their size, rather than being slightly handicapped by it. Shaquille was already incredibly agile, but he was eager to receive any coaching that people wanted to offer, especially when it came to improving his offensive abilities.

After Big Man Camp, it was time for Shaquille

to go to the Magic's pre-season training camp. Pre-season training camps serve as a sort of spring training — in the early fall — to help players get back into shape, study the playbook the coaching staff has assembled for the upcoming season, and learn any new offensive or defensive strategies the coaches have devised. Training camp is also the best opportunity for players to get to know one another on an informal basis, without the pressures of the regular season getting in the way. A professional basketball team carries twelve players on its regular squad, and due to injuries, the draft, trades, free agency, and retirements, there is quite a lot of turnover every year. The better players get to know one another, and become used to each other's individual strengths and weaknesses, the easier it is to form a winning team.

Shaquille was only a rookie, but he was already considered the foundation of the Magic's future. That meant that he had to be careful to strike a balance between healthy confidence and rookie humility. Veterans prefer it when a rookie "knows his place," but a rookie as gifted as Shaquille is given a lot more leeway.

So many people wanted to catch a glimpse of Orlando's new franchise star that the Magic decided it would be less distracting if they moved their training-camp site out of town. Otherwise, the area would be so crowded with fans and the media that the team wouldn't be able to get any work done. The Magic decided on a site in the town of Deland, which was well outside of Orlando, and then the players and coaches settled down to get ready for the new season.

Orlando's head coach was Matt Guokas, who had been coaching the Magic since their first season in the NBA three years earlier, and he was thrilled to have his new center. With Shaquille anchoring the team, the Magic would be treated as a serious contender for the first time in their existence. A new franchise often has trouble earning respect from the better-established teams, but with one pick, the Magic now had it.

In their first exhibition game, against the Miami Heat, Shaquille made some rookie mistakes, including causing nine turnovers. Then, in their second game against the Charlotte Hornets, Shaquille relaxed a little, and delivered a 26 point, 11 rebound performance. He still made too many turnovers, but Coach Guokas and the Magic were delighted by what they were seeing.

Shaquille really *was* their star of the future.

6
Shaquille Plays for Real

The night of Shaquille's first professional game, all of Orlando was eagerly awaiting the debut of their young phenom. The arena was completely sold out, and ready to cheer their Magic on.

In their three years as a franchise, the Orlando Magic had never had a winning season, and their record in the 1991–1992 season had been a sub-par 21 wins and 61 losses. Obviously, the powerhouse teams of the NBA hadn't been losing any sleep over playing the Magic. But this year, everyone from Orlando coach Matt Guokas to the people selling popcorn in the stands hoped that things would be different.

Potentially, Orlando's starting lineup was very good. With Shaquille anchoring the team at center, and Scott Skiles acting as the spark plug at point guard, the rest of the Magic's hopes were pinned on three-point threat Dennis Scott and explosive scorer Nick Anderson being able to play with consistency, and make it through the season injury free — problems each of them had had the season before. Veterans Terry Catledge and Jeff Turner were likely to split most of the time at the other forward position, although power forward was still the team's weakest position. Brian Williams was still struggling to adjust to life in the NBA, both personally and professionally, and not having much success.

The first game of the new season was against the Magic's closest — geographically and otherwise — rival, the Miami Heat. The Heat, headlined by center Rony Seikaly and forward Glen Rice, were another new franchise, struggling to compete with the more-established teams like the Knicks and the Celtics.

The sell-out crowd of 15,151 cheered wildly at the first tip-off, and then settled back to watch the game. Shaquille started off a little slow, but brought the first quarter to a dramatic close with a huge dunk. Shaquille's game continued to be on the uneven side, as he scored only 12 points, but he grabbed a team-high 18 rebounds, including five offensive boards. He blocked an impressive three shots, but displayed some rookie nerves by committing eight turnovers.

In the meantime, Nick Anderson was busy scoring a whopping 42 points, while Dennis Scott added 27 of his own, including four three-point shots in only five attempts. Shaquille fouled out, late in the fourth quarter, but by then, his teammates had the game well in hand, and the Magic came away with their first victory of the year, beating the Heat, 110–100.

For now, at least, they were in first place.

With those initial jitters behind him, Shaquille was eager for the team's next game against another Atlantic Division rival, the Washington Bullets. He played with more confidence, scoring 22 points, and yanked down 15 rebounds to pace the Magic in both categories, although five of his teammates scored in double figures, too.

Shaquille also blocked four shots, three of them coming in the crucial closing minutes of the game, and the Magic posted a solid 103–98 victory.

The Magic's next outing was against the Central Division's Charlotte Hornets, yet another of the newer franchises. The Hornets were an up-and-coming team, with both Shaquille's former college rival, center Alonzo Mourning, and the first pick from the 1991 NBA draft, Larry Johnson, on their roster.

Shaquille started off hot, scoring 20 points in the first half, and then adding another 15 in the third quarter. But in the fourth quarter, he didn't score any points at all, and with Nick Anderson having an off-night with only 12 points, the team was unable to hold off the pesky Hornets, who strolled away with a win.

Two days later, the Magic regrouped for another game against the Bullets, winning by a lopsided score of 127–100. Shaquille ruled the night — again — with 31 points and an awesome 21 rebounds, but Dennis Scott, Nick Anderson, and Scott Skiles were right behind him, with 27, 25, and 14 points, respectively. Skiles, always a scrappy player, even pitched in with a surprising 12 rebounds. All told, the Magic had 69 rebounds, compared to only 34 for the Bullets, and a team that controls the boards will almost always win the game.

So, after just four games, Shaquille was averaging 25 points and almost 17 rebounds. He became the only rookie *ever* to be selected as the NBA Player of the Week in his first week as a professional. Anyone who had had any doubts about Shaquille being "the real deal" didn't have them anymore.

"He's the most celebrated player who's ever come into the league," *Orlando Sentinel* reporter Tim Povtak, who covers the Magic regularly, observed. "This guy, in his rookie season, has been anointed the next great star. He's unique in sports history because there's never been anyone in *any* sport who's been this big — 7'1", three hundred pounds — who's also this athletic. Basically, he's still a kid, but he doesn't *play* his age."

Next, the Magic went on the road to play two more division rivals, the New Jersey Nets, and the Philadelphia 76ers. They lost both games, despite Shaquille's big numbers. His play against the 76ers was particularly impressive as he came up with 38 points, 16 rebounds, and an eye-

50

opening — and ego-deflating, for the other team — eight blocked shots. He got into foul trouble in each of the games, but at least managed to foul out two different New Jersey Nets centers to keep him company.

The traveling schedule in the NBA is very hectic, and no sooner had the Magic finished their game with Philadelphia than they had to fly back to Orlando to play the Golden State Warriors. Golden State was leading after the first half, but Shaquille, the "little warrior," and his teammates banged in 40 points in the third quarter and never looked back, sending the Warriors away with a 126–102 shellacking.

Orlando was off to their best start in franchise history, and with a record of five wins and only two defeats, were in first place in the Atlantic Division. Nick Anderson and Dennis Scott were playing almost as well as Shaquille was, with the three players combining for over 70 points a game. Scott Skiles was contributing his always-steady efforts, and players like Anthony Bowie, Donald Royal, and Jeff Turner were adding solid support, despite fairly limited playing time.

The Magic's next game was against the New York Knicks, and it would be Shaquille's first chance to play against one of the premier centers in the game, as he matched up against perpetual All-Star Patrick Ewing. Knicks coach Pat Riley had benched three of his fiery young players, John Starks, Anthony Mason, and Greg Anthony, in an attempt to improve their attitudes, but the Magic were unable to take advantage of the situation, scoring only 77 points, their lowest total of the season. The Knicks scored only 92 points, but that was more than enough to win.

Shaquille played his hardest against Patrick, and although it would have been difficult for anyone to avoid being nervous while appearing in the fabled Madison Square Garden for the first time, Shaquille didn't show it. The Knicks are known for their overpowering defense, and they double-teamed Shaquille more often than not, holding him to 18 points and forcing him to make seven turnovers. Nick Anderson was able to take some of the pressure off by scoring 27 points, but the Knicks were just too tough down the stretch.

Just looking at the numbers, Shaquille out-played Patrick Ewing, with 18 points to Patrick's 15, and 17 rebounds to Patrick's nine — but he would rather have won the game.

After the loss in New York, the Magic finished the month of November on a high note, with victories against the Houston Rockets, the Indiana Pacers, and the Cleveland Cavaliers. Shaquille had a poor game against Houston, but Scott Skiles came up big with 30 points, and 11 assists, and Dennis Scott added 28 points. So even though Shaquille was out-dueled by the Rockets' star center, Hakeem Olajuwon, the Magic won easily.

Scott Skiles also took charge in the game against the Pacers, with 32 points, adding another 28 the next night against Cleveland. Over an eighty-two-game season, players are going to have ups and downs, and no team can win with only one star. It was a very good sign for the Magic's future that Shaquille wasn't being forced to deliver night after night, and that his teammates were able to take turns carrying the team when he couldn't.

After the first month of the season, the Magic were still in first place, a position that would have seemed unthinkable a year earlier. So far, Shaquille was living up to all the pre-season hype — and more.

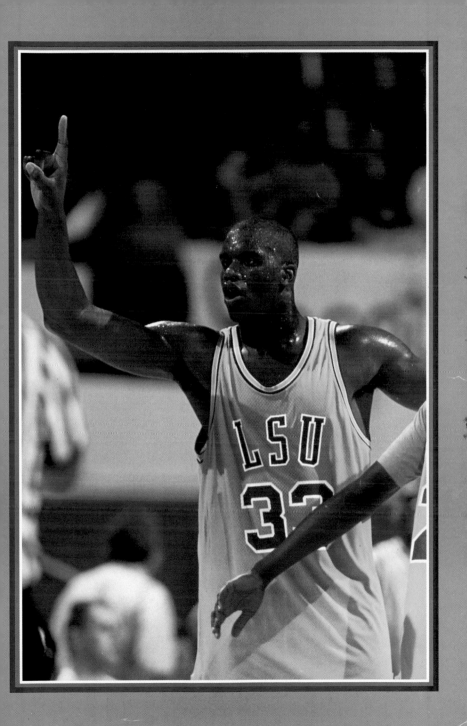

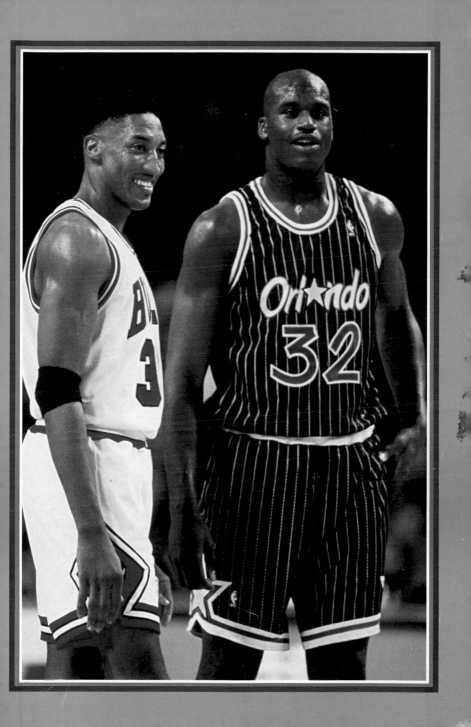

7
The Changing of the Guard

One of the reasons that Shaquille has exploded onto the scene unlike any athlete anyone can ever remember is that right now, the NBA is in a period of great transition. What is happening is a sort of changing of the guard.

Back in the late seventies, fan interest in professional basketball had dropped off to its lowest level ever. In fact, several franchises were even in danger of going out of business. Major league baseball and the NFL were dominating the American sports imagination — and NBA basketball was now the ugly duckling of the professional sports world.

Then, everything changed when two new young stars named Magic Johnson and Larry Bird came along. They were friends; they were rivals; they were *stars*. Suddenly, people were watching basketball again, and children who once had gone outside to field grounders were now going out to shoot hoops.

The NBA was well on its way to regaining popularity when another player showed up and changed basketball forever. His name was Michael Jordan. Michael could do things with a ball, and in the air, that no one had ever seen before. He became a superstar, and perhaps the most recognizable and best-liked athlete in the world. In just ten years, the NBA went from earning barely over 100 million dollars a year to *700* million.

Now the players were idolized, the championships were thrilling, and everyone associated with the NBA was delighted. The NBA's growth potential seemed to be without any limitations.

But unfortunately, nothing lasts forever, and by the end of the 1991–92 season, both Larry Bird and Magic Johnson had been forced to retire prematurely. Larry Bird had sustained a back injury that would no longer allow him to play — or even get through life — pain-free, and Magic Johnson had stunned the world when he announced that he had tested positive for the HIV virus, and would be leaving the game.

The combination of losing those two great players, and the fact that Michael Jordan was beginning to talk about quitting in the next few years, made the NBA's hold on a booming financial future suddenly seem tenuous. Somewhere, somehow, the league needed a *new* star. They needed a star who was not only an athlete with stratospheric talents, but one who was also likable and charming. They needed an athlete who even nonfans would recognize and enjoy. A star like that only shows up about once every decade and the NBA needed one — right away.

There were a number of young players who seemed promising, like Larry Johnson, Derrick Coleman, Steve Smith, and Jimmy Jackson, but none of them had really captured the public's interest yet.

When NBA officials heard the distinctive and instantly memorable name Shaquille O'Neal, they saw the future. They had found a giant twenty-year-old center whose smiles into the camera were as sweet as his slam-dunks were fierce. Here was a player who was bigger, and stronger, and *younger* than anyone else in the league. Without a doubt, a star was waiting to be born.

Madison Avenue recognized Shaquille's star quality, too, and before the season had even started, Shaquille was already receiving lucrative endorsement offers from companies eager to sign up this great new talent. After carefully mulling over each offer with his agent, Shaquille accepted a number of them, lifting himself from the category of multi-millionaire to multi-multi-millionaire. Shaquille was showing an unprecedented level of marketability for a player who had yet to play a single minute of basketball as a professional.

Almost all star athletes select a sneaker company to endorse, and Shaquille signed on with Reebok, who developed a special high-top sneaker — in size 20, triple E — called the Shaq Attaq. Shaquille's mammoth sneakers are a full sixteen inches long, and close to six inches wide. Shaquille was going to be the youngest player in the NBA — but he had the biggest feet of anyone since Hall of Famer Bob Lanier, who had worn size 22 sneakers. Shaquille's five-year contract with Reebok was estimated to be worth three million dollars a year, which would put him second only to Michael Jordan in the shoe endorsement category.

"We're really ecstatic about the relationship," Reebok representative Dave Fogelson said in a recent interview. "He's an athlete who kind of transcends the basketball category. He's a person who likes to have fun, and doesn't seem to get too wrapped up in any of the money, or celebrity status. Beyond the statistics, we like the personality and enthusiasm he's exuded, both on and off the court."

Shaquille's series of commercials for Reebok are memorable, with tag lines like "Don't fake the funk on a nasty dunk." That sort of remark is classic Shaq-speak, wherein nobody knows quite what it means, but they like hearing it, anyway. In one of the commercials, Shaquille enters a darkened basketball court, where a group of the most legendary centers in basketball history, men like Wilt Chamberlain and Bill Russell, are waiting for him. Shaquille shatters the backboard with a crushing dunk, and turns to receive his elders' praise. Instead, they hold out a broom and dustpan for him to clean up the mess. Shaquille frowns, and asks, "Is this a rookie thing?"

In another commercial, the great centers recite a poem to him, with Shaquille's father, Sergeant Harrison, giving his son the last "And which is more, you'll be a man, my son" line. Shaquille smiles, and sales soar.

Shaquille also signed endorsement contracts with several other companies, including Pepsi, Kenner, and Spalding. Certainly, no athlete had come along in years who had had this much immediate commercial appeal.

"We've been involved with some of the premier basketball stars of the past twenty years," Spalding representative Scott Dickey explained in an interview. "Julius Erving, Larry Bird, Magic Johnson — some of the true leaders of the professional sport of basketball. We like people who can be ambassadors for the game, not only from a performance standpoint, but also in the way they live their lives off the court. That's very important, in terms of marketing an athlete who is endorsing our products. It was obvious to us that Shaquille is a perfect role model for kids."

For Spalding, Shaquille agreed to lend his name to a line of "Shaq Attaq" basketballs and Shaquille O'Neal backboards.

"*Unbreakable* backboards," Scott Dickey promised, with a laugh. "Shaq-proof."

Shaquille's campaign for Pepsi has spawned another group of crowd-pleasing commercials. For example, in one commercial set on a city playground, Shaquille reaches up and pulls down a backboard mounted on a solid metal pole. When the hoop is at a more comfortable chest-level height, Shaquille slams the ball through the hoop. This super-hero feat makes him thirsty, and he looks around until he finds a small boy holding a Pepsi. "Don't even *think* about it," the boy says, and grins.

Shaq-mania has become so extreme that a number of people have broken the law in order to obtain memorabilia. Sports cards have become a very big business in recent years, and Shaquille's cards have nearly taken over the marketplace. When McDonald's restaurants ran a promotion giving away Upper Deck basketball cards, four people in Florida were arrested — in two separate cases — for stealing Shaquille O'Neal cards, which they would then sell for as much as forty-five dollars *each*. Someone else made counterfeit versions of the Shaquille O'Neal Lottery Pick card, and was getting as much as *two hundred* dollars for each one until the authorities caught on. Two more men were arrested at a card show after stealing two hundred Shaquille O'Neal cards, in a Topps version that was worth up to two hundred and fifty dollars apiece. You know an athlete is popular when even *criminals* like him.

As far as Shaquille's personal life is concerned,

he is recognized everywhere he goes, and is asked to sign autographs and pose for pictures. Some professional athletes can go places and be ignored, but basketball players are so much *taller* than everyone else that they have a harder time passing unnoticed. So far, Shaquille has given every indication that he enjoys the spotlight. Since he loves rap music, and is an honorary member of the Fu-Schnickens, he may become a celebrity within the music world, too. He spends a lot of time writing and rapping songs of his own, and has dropped hints that a second career may be in his future. If he is even remotely as successful as he has been as a basketball player, MTV will have to set up a new category for Shaq Awards.

Without a doubt, Shaquille's transition from college junior to national sports superstar has been lightning-quick, and barring injury, he should help to ensure the NBA's popularity for at least the next decade. But even with the excitement of all the media attention, Shaquille knew that he had to concentrate on his most important priority — helping the Orlando Magic win basketball games.

8
You Win Some, You Lose Some

The Magic began December with their first trip out to the West Coast. Since they didn't play very well, the highlight of Shaquille's trip was definitely his appearance on *The Arsenio Hall Show*. While there, he performed with the Fu-Schnickens, making it obvious that he is just as comfortable holding a microphone as he is with a basketball in his hands.

"When the television cameras go on, he loves it," *Orlando Sentinel* reporter Tim Povtak said later. "The more cameras, the better. He *likes* the limelight."

Dave Fogelson, who works with Shaquille at Reebok, agreed completely. "He's a natural in front of the camera," he said. "He's been described in a lot of different ways, but with his love of rap music and the appeal he has to younger people, he really is a hero for the nineties."

On the court though, Shaquille had less fun that week. Against the Seattle SuperSonics, he scored only nine points, missing six out of seven foul shots. Shooting free throws was still by far the weakest part of Shaquille's game.

After losing to Seattle, the Magic played the Los Angeles Clippers, and Shaquille went up against his old LSU teammate Stanley Roberts. Shaquille held him to only 16 points and six rebounds, while scoring 26 points of his own, but the Magic still lost 122–104. Ken Norman had a big game for the Clippers, with 33 points, and Clipper guard Ron Harper was four-for-five from three-point territory.

Shaquille and his teammates were hoping to salvage one win from their road trip, but Golden State got some revenge on their home turf, after having lost to the Magic earlier in Orlando. The Warriors won handily, 119–104, and the Magic came limping back to Florida, hoping to improve their fortunes.

Despite being back on familiar ground, the Magic's losing streak continued. Behind Reggie Lewis and Kevin Gamble, the Boston Celtics dominated the game, winning 117–102. Shaquille scored 26 points and snagged 15 rebounds, but in typical fashion, the Celtics got hot in the fourth quarter when Kevin Gamble came off the bench and made ten of his twelve shots.

The game against Boston was the first chance

Shaquille, the youngest player in the league, had had to play against Robert Parish, the oldest player in the NBA. Once again, as in the game against Patrick Ewing, Shaquille had better numbers, but his opponent went home with a win.

Having lost four games in a row, the Magic had now dropped to third place in the Atlantic Division, behind the Knicks and the Nets — and things only got worse. The Magic flew to Detroit to play the Pistons, and despite their best efforts, lost again. Detroit defensive master Dennis Rodman put on a rebounding show, pulling down 22, which was twice as many as Shaquille had. Guard Joe Dumars scored 39 points, with 13 in the last three and a half minutes of the game, to pace the Pistons.

The only really good thing that happened in the game for the Magic was that they made 14 three-point shots, which was a new team record. Dennis Scott sent up eight of those efforts, and finished with 38 points on the night, but the Magic still fell short, by a score of 108–103.

The next team they had to face was the dangerous Phoenix Suns, who were on a five-game winning streak to match the Magic's losing streak. Shaquille scored 26 points, but after being fouled twice with only a few seconds left in the game, missed two of his four foul shots, either one of which would have tied the game. If he had made all *four* shots, the Magic would have won — but he didn't. Even a player as good as Shaquille can't *always* deliver in the clutch, and once again,

Shaquille's poor free-throw shooting had come back to haunt him.

By now, the Magic had lost six games in a row, and it seemed as though there was no end in sight. But Coach Guokas kept his team's spirits up, and after taking advantage of the off-weekend in their schedule, the Magic started off furiously in their next game. They were playing the 76ers at home, and they scored 40 points in the first quarter and never looked back. Shaquille blocked six shots, to go along with his 20 points and 14 rebounds, and Dennis Scott, Nick Anderson, and Jeff Turner all scored over 20 points apiece. The Magic won 119–107, and the terrible losing streak was finally over.

With the season almost a quarter over, Shaquille was ranked eleventh in the league in scoring with a 22.4 points-per-game average. As usual, Michael Jordan, of the Chicago Bulls, was leading the league with a 32.8 points-per-game mark. In the rebounding category, Shaquille was second in the NBA behind Detroit's Dennis Rodman, averaging 14.8 rebounds a game. The Magic might only be playing .500 ball, but Shaquille certainly wasn't playing like anyone's definition of a *rookie*.

The Magic continued their winning ways against the Sacramento Kings, with Shaquille getting more rebounds than the entire Kings team *combined*. Orlando followed up on that victory by going on the road and trouncing the Atlanta Hawks by a 125–84 score. It was the second worst defeat the Hawks had ever faced on their home court, and the Magic accomplished it by solid teamwork and steady shooting, up and down the entire lineup. Shaquille's numbers were somewhat lackluster, but the rest of the Magic made up for that, led by Dennis Scott's 26 points.

Three days later, against Karl Malone and the Utah Jazz, Shaquille ran into foul trouble in the second half. While he was on the bench, the Magic lost their lead, and Shaquille was only able to watch in frustration. Once Coach Guokas put him back in the game, Shaquille played with wild energy, helping the Magic run off 14 points, while the Jazz scored only three. Shaquille finished the night with 28 points, 19 rebounds, and five blocked shots, and the Magic went home with yet another win.

With four victories in a row, the Magic were feeling pretty good, but the Miami Heat took the wind out of their sails a few nights later, beating them 106–100. It was a game the Magic really shouldn't have lost, since Heat center Rony Seikaly was injured and unable to play, but rookie Harold Miner picked up the slack, scoring six unexpected points in the final minute and a half of the game to assure Miami's win. Shaquille ran into foul trouble again, spending vital minutes languishing on the bench while Miami controlled the ball at both ends of the court, and ultimately, the game.

Rather than dwelling on their loss, the Magic

came back to beat the Milwaukee Bucks at home, 110–94. They had a total of 11 blocked shots, only five of which were Shaquille's, and Dennis Scott paced the squad with 20 points, including five three-pointers.

Now, the Magic had only one more game to play in 1992. They were facing the Los Angeles Lakers, who were still adjusting to playing without Magic Johnson, but the Lakers won, anyway. Shaquille dominated the boards with 23 rebounds and scored 23 points to go along with Nick Anderson's 30, but Sam Perkins came off the bench for the Lakers to score nine fourth-quarter points, and the Lakers won 96–93.

After two months of the season, the Magic were still stuck in third place behind New York and New Jersey, with 13 wins against 11 defeats. They were playing well, but Shaquille wanted to play even *better*.

9
A Shaq Attaq

Shaquille and the Magic started off on the wrong foot by losing their first game to the Pistons, despite the fact that Shaquille scored 29 points, and had 15 rebounds. The game was very close, but the Pistons hung on, 98–97.

Shaquille was playing like a seasoned pro, but he was still finding that his two biggest weaknesses were continuing to plague him — free-throw shooting, and committing too many fouls of his own, which resulted in him wasting long, frustrating minutes sitting on the bench.

The only way Shaquille would ever be able to improve his shooting percentage from the line would be by devoting many more hours of practice time to working on that one skill, but it would be hours well spent. Since all of the opposing teams knew that Shaquille's free-throw shooting was weak, they often used the strategy of fouling him at crucial moments of the game and forcing him to score from the line, instead of under the basket where he was more comfortable. Improving his shooting skills would take away one of the few weapons other teams had to contain him.

On the other hand, staying out of foul trouble is almost always a problem for big frontcourt players like centers and power forwards. When players at these positions are aggressive with their defense and rebounding, there tends to be a lot of bumping and banging into other players, and referees are quick to blow their whistles to keep the game under control. It is also easy for a referee to assume that a player as big as Shaquille is generally going to be the one *doing* all of the bumping, not the one receiving it. Shaquille probably wasn't going to get the benefit of the doubt very often, but he would have to accept that as a given and work around the situation.

The most important thing a great center needs to learn is not to give up *easy*, or silly, fouls. If a player gets flustered by being surrounded by too many defenders, he may throw an unnecessary elbow, and if he loses his temper, he is likely to push back more roughly than referees will allow. A great center learns when to back off, and when to bear down. With experience, he even learns that there are times, especially in close games, when it is *good* to give up a foul, rather than allow an opponent to make a shot uncontested. Over the next couple of years, Shaquille will only get better at making those sorts of split-second decisions.

When a team like the Magic has a player as obviously gifted as Shaquille is, opposing teams are likely to concentrate most of their efforts on containing him. Guarding a star one-on-one is unrealistic because that almost always means that the star will be able to shoot at will. Therefore, teams tend to collapse their defenders around this dangerous scoring threat, double — or even triple — teaming him. When this happens, a player is likely to get nervous and rush his shots, or turn the ball over. But what Shaquille had to remember was that if he was being guarded by more than one player at a time, that would always mean that at least one of his teammates was *not* being guarded. So, it's important for a center to keep his cool, look around for the open man, and get the ball to him.

The Magic played their second game of the new year against the New Jersey Nets. While Shaquille scored almost 30 points, Derrick Coleman managed to cancel him out by scoring the same, and also out-rebounded him. By challenging him repeatedly, driving toward the basket, Derrick was able to get Shaquille to commit four fouls by the third quarter, and he was stuck on the bench until halfway through the fourth quarter. After coming back in, Shaquille played hard, but ultimately fouled out, and the Nets prevailed.

After losing that game, the Magic had to face the Atlantic Division-leading Knicks next. The

Knicks played well, and were holding a ten-point lead with only six minutes left in the game. Shaquille and his teammates could have given up, but they fought back. Shaquille had been on the bench with four fouls, but when he returned to the floor, he helped the Magic score 14 points, while New York managed only three. Shaquille had a lot to do with that low total, as he blocked *two* of Patrick Ewing's shots during that run.

With less than a minute to play, Dennis Scott sent his fourth three-pointer swishing through the net, giving the Magic a one-point lead. With just seconds left, Knicks guard John Starks passed the ball to Patrick Ewing. Shaquille was right on top of him, and Patrick missed a quick hook shot. Shaquille grabbed the rebound, and held onto the ball as the game ended. Patrick protested that he had been fouled, but the referees disagreed, and Shaquille and the Magic had a dramatic last-second victory against the Knicks, 95–94.

The team faced the less dominating Indiana Pacers the next night and, as often happens after an exciting win, they were somewhat drained — and played that way. Shaquille had one of his better games of the season, pounding the boards for 20 rebounds, blocking eight shots, and scoring 30 points, but none of his teammates could do the same. The Magic made 18 turnovers, and missed all nine of the three-point shots they attempted, while six Indiana players, led by Reggie Miller and Dale Davis, scored in double figures.

It was another one of those games that proved that a team needs more than one spectacular performance and one star to win. No matter how well Shaquille played on any given night, if Nick Anderson and the other Magic players didn't also shoot and score, the game was not likely to turn out in their favor. The best recent example of this phenomenon is probably Michael Jordan and the Chicago Bulls. Michael was a brilliant star from the moment he put on an NBA uniform, but until players like Scottie Pippen and Horace Grant began to deliver on a regular basis, the Bulls never went anywhere. Michael could score 50 points every night, but the team didn't become a real powerhouse until they started producing as a *team*. The Magic needed to follow that example.

And now two of the Magic's next three games were against those very same NBA champion Bulls, one at home and the other in Chicago.

During the first game, the Magic trailed by only three points at halftime, and looked to be in pretty good shape as Nick Anderson was shooting well to back up Shaquille. But then, in the third quarter, the Bulls turned on the heat, and the Magic were way behind before even realizing what had happened. The final score of 122–106 looked closer than it actually was.

Ironically, neither Shaquille nor Michael really dominated the game, scoring only 19 and 23 points respectively. But while the Bulls blocked seven shots, the Magic didn't block *any*, and they committed 20 turnovers. Bulls Scottie Pippen and Horace Grant were the real heroes of the night, as Scottie came up with a triple-double game, and Horace scored 26 points, making a remarkable 12 of the 15 shots he attempted.

After that, the Magic flew up to Boston, where they beat the Celtics handily, and then went on to Chicago for a rematch. This time, even though Michael Jordan stole the show by scoring 64 points — more than anyone in the NBA had scored in a game all season — the Magic went back to their hotel happy, as they won 128–124.

Shaquille had a great game with 29 points and 24 big rebounds, while Scott Skiles sparked the team with 31 points of his own. Although the Magic had been losing late in the game, they rallied and Nick Anderson made a clutch three-pointer to tie the score. Orlando controlled the game the rest of the way, winning in overtime. It is hard enough to beat the Bulls *anywhere*, but beating them on their home court, in overtime, is a great achievement. Shaquille could also be especially pleased that he had committed only two fouls during fifty minutes of playing time, and so was able to be on the floor when his team needed him.

The Magic might not be ready to win an NBA championship yet, but at least they were starting to knock on the door.

During the next few weeks, the Magic played like a person repeatedly taking two steps forward, and then two steps backward. They would win two games, and then lose two, win two, and lose two more. So they weren't falling further back in the Atlantic Division, but they weren't gaining any ground either. It didn't help matters that three-point ace Dennis Scott was fighting leg injuries, and unable to play most of the time.

Some nights, Shaquille would run the show, scoring as many as 38 points; other nights, he would only come up with 18 or 20. That would seem almost disappointing, even though scoring 20 points is very good. Barely halfway into his first season, it was already easy to take Shaquille's consistently outstanding performances for granted.

But win or lose, Shaquille was still the center of attention as far as the media and fans were concerned. Night after night, the Orlando Arena was selling out. In previous seasons, the Magic had been one of the least popular teams to see when they were on the road; now, attendance at their games was second only to Michael Jordan and the Chicago Bulls. In each new NBA city, a ticket to see Shaquille play was one of the hottest in town.

That kind of scrutiny can be hard to handle, but Shaquille seemed to thrive on the attention.

"At this point, he still enjoys it," *Orlando Sentinel* reporter Tim Povtak said. "Other guys have come into the league with a lot of hoopla, and shied away from all of the publicity, but I think he's unique. There are some players who they say would play just as well if there was nobody in the arena, but he's not like that. And compared to any other athlete I've been around at this age, he's handled it very well."

Shaquille had exciting news when the final results of the All-Star voting were tabulated, and it turned out that he was the first rookie since Michael Jordan to be voted to the starting lineup in the game. Shaquille received 826,767 votes, far outdistancing the traditional winner at the center position, Patrick Ewing, who ended up with 578,368 votes. The only players in the entire league who received more votes than Shaquille were Michael Jordan, who tallied more than a million votes, Scottie Pippen, with over 900,000, and Charles Barkley, with more than 850,000. Being in the starting lineup with the best the NBA had to offer was going to be a great honor.

In the meantime, Shaquille tried to help the Magic win. In spite of their best efforts, Orlando just couldn't seem to get out of fourth place. Anthony Bowie had been filling in admirably in Dennis Scott's absence, but even with Nick Anderson's great shooting abilities, the team was really hurting without the presence of a viable three-point threat. Opposing defenses were able to stay in on Shaquille, knowing that the Magic's outside shooting wasn't strong enough to hurt them. So Orlando would lose games that a more versatile team would have won.

Early in February, the Magic were on national television for the first time of the season, playing Charles Barkley and the Phoenix Suns. The Magic ended up losing, and Shaquille struggled with foul troubles throughout, but anyone who watched the game only remembered one thing. In his national debut, Shaquille not only broke the backboard while slamming in a dunk — but knocked down the entire apparatus, delaying the game for over half an hour while the unit was replaced. The force of his dunk had caused the whole contraption to sink slowly, inexorably, down onto the floor, like a movie special effect. And it *was* special — it was a Shaq Attaq!

10
Rookie Reminders

Without a doubt, Shaquille knew how to make a dramatic entrance on the national NBA scene, although there were cynical viewers who suspected that the backboard had been rigged. Of course, this wasn't true, but the networks knew a good thing when they saw it, and a week after the game with Phoenix, the Magic appeared on national television again. This time, they were playing the Knicks, which gave the commentators plenty of material as they analyzed various aspects of the Shaquille O'Neal/Patrick Ewing matchup. So far, Shaquille had always played well against Patrick, but the Magic were still considered the underdog. To make matters worse, the Knicks were in the middle of a seven-game winning streak, and were giving the impression that they might never lose again.

To the network's delight, the game went into triple-overtime, with both teams battling away during every second. Shaquille didn't break anything — not even a record — but it was the first nationally televised game to go into triple-overtime in years. Seventeen years, to be precise.

Both teams missed many more shots than they made, with shooting percentages below .350, and Knicks guard John Starks alone took 36 shots, making only 10 of them. Shaquille's shooting hand was pretty cold, too, as he made only eight of 25 attempts.

At the end of the first half, the Magic were winning 39–34, which was the lowest number of points either team had scored during one half all season. Shaquille and Patrick each ran into foul problems, but the more experienced Ewing was still able to score 34 points to Shaquille's 21. However, Shaquille topped Patrick in both rebounds and blocked shots, tallying a stupendous total of nine blocked shots to Patrick's four. If he had rejected just one more ball, Shaquille would have ended up with a triple-double game — a rare achievement, even at the professional level.

The Knicks had a good chance to win the game during regulation time, since they had a five-point lead with only forty seconds to play, but the Magic were able to tie the score. So, the teams went to their first overtime. With just 13.7 seconds left, Patrick fouled out, and Shaquille rose to the occasion by sinking both free throws. The Knicks hurt themselves by missing more than half of their own free throws, and compounded their problems when forwards Charles Oakley and Charles Smith also fouled out and had to join Patrick on the bench.

During the final two overtimes, Shaquille blocked a staggering four shots, including one lofted by John Starks that would have won the game at the end of the second overtime. Another one, attempted by backup center Herb Williams, would have tied the score.

To cap off his evening, it was Shaquille who scored the winning basket, giving Herb Williams a quick fake and then sliding past him to flick the ball up. It slipped through the net, and the Magic had won the most dramatic game in the history of their franchise, leaving the Knicks, and the fans at Madison Square Garden, devastated.

For the second time that season, Shaquille and his teammates had beaten one of the premier teams in the NBA, on their home court, in relentlessly dramatic fashion.

The future for Shaquille and the Magic was looking very bright.

A letdown after that great victory seemed inevitable, and Orlando lost their next game to Detroit, albeit after going into overtime. A glance at the box score would suggest that Shaquille had had his best game yet, scoring 46 points and snagging 21 rebounds, but in fact, his problems at the foul line resurfaced. He missed one free throw that kept the Magic from winning the game outright, and then missed four more during the over-time period. Once again, it was easy to see which aspect of Shaquille's overall game needed the most improvement. Of course, the fact that he had so many strengths also helped make his few weaknesses seem so blatant.

The Magic bounced back in their final game before the All-Star break against the Denver Nuggets, winning 111–96, although Shaquille's old friend from LSU, Chris Jackson, had a big night for Denver, scoring 25 points. Since, so far, Chris had not had the success in his professional career that people had predicted, it was nice for Shaquille to see his friend do well — as long as the Magic brought home a win.

Now it was time for Shaquille to go to the All-Star Game, which was being held in Salt Lake City, to take his place among the best of the best in the NBA.

Every professional player dreams of being selected to the All-Star team. For one thing, it is a very big honor, but players also like having the opportunity to play with other athletes they admire. The All-Star Game tends to be on the informal side, and players enjoy being able to treat one another as friends, rather than opponents.

The four other starters voted to the Eastern Conference team along with Shaquille were Michael Jordan, Larry Johnson, Scottie Pippen, and Isiah Thomas. The East team was being coached by Knicks coach Pat Riley, and the rest of the players chosen for the team were Patrick Ewing, Joe Dumars, Mark Price, Brad Daugherty, Dominique Wilkins, Larry Nance, and Detlef Schrempf.

The Western Conference team starters were Clyde Drexler, John Stockton, Charles Barkley, Karl Malone, and center David Robinson. The other players selected to represent the West were Dan Majerle, Danny Manning, Hakeem Olajuwon, Tim Hardaway, Terry Porter, Shawn Kemp, and Sean Elliott.

It was exhilarating for Shaquille, as the only rookie, to be playing in the same game with so many elite stars. Most of the other players had been on the All-Star team in the past, although it was the first time in many years that neither the Los Angeles Lakers nor the Boston Celtics were represented. The Larry Bird/Magic Johnson days really were over, and the new Shaquille/*Larry* Johnson days were beginning.

To Shaquille's dismay, East team coach Pat Riley decided to give most of the playing time at center to Patrick Ewing, using the logic that Shaquille could look forward to many years of being an All-Star, but that it wasn't time for Patrick to step aside just yet. Shaquille took this with good grace, although it wasn't much fun to spend half of the game on the bench, playing only a brief stint in the fourth quarter. But he *did* get to play for twenty-five minutes all told, scoring 14 points, with seven rebounds. During the overtime, he and Patrick were *both* on the court, although Shaquille wasn't able to score or pull down any rebounds.

Shaquille tried to play his usual jamming, slamming game throughout, but against such tough competition, he wasn't as successful as usual. In fact, he was rejected more than once, both by David Robinson and Karl Malone. Since Karl Malone was later given co-MVP honors, along with his Utah teammate point guard John Stockton, that may have taken some of the sting out of Shaquille having his shot blocked, but it was still a little embarrassing.

So while being an All-Star was fun, Shaquille was also reminded, repeatedly, that even though he was a great player, he was still — a rookie. Since he was just happy to have been selected, Shaquille didn't argue the point.

When the game was over, the West team had beaten the East team, 135–132. The fans had had fun, the players had had fun, and Shaquille had every intention of earning the right to come back and do it again every year.

After the All-Star break, the Magic fell back into their old habit of winning one game, and then losing the next. Eight teams from each conference go to the playoffs every year, and while the Magic were still in the hunt, they were going to have to put together some wins if they were going to make it. The Knicks, the Nets, the Bulls, and the Cavaliers were all sure bets to win playoff spots, but the other four slots were still up for grabs. Shaquille wanted very much for his team to grab one of them.

As of early March, Shaquille was still ranked second in the NBA in rebounding behind Detroit's Dennis Rodman, and he was seventh in the NBA in scoring, with a 23.9 point-per-game average. Shaquille also held the third spot in field goal percentage, behind the Cavaliers' Brad Daugherty and Dale Davis of Indiana, and he was third in the blocked shots category, trailing Hakeem Olajuwon and Alonzo Mourning.

Somehow, Shaquille's name wasn't showing up anywhere on the free-throw percentage list.

By the end of the month, seven of the eight playoff spots in the Eastern Conference had been decided, and the Magic were one and a half games behind the Indiana Pacers for the final spot. Every game was a big game now.

On March 27, the Magic beat the New Jersey Nets to gain their thirty-second win of the season. It was the first time Orlando had beaten New Jersey all season long, but more importantly, thirty-two games were more than the Magic had *ever* won in one season.

As usual, Shaquille was the top scorer for his team with 27 points, but five other members of the Magic also scored in double figures. Shaquille took charge of the game in the final minutes, scoring eight points in a row to help his team build an insurmountable lead. He also stole the ball five times during the game, which tied the record for a Magic rookie. Just to keep things interesting, he also came up with 17 rebounds and three blocked shots. All of this made up for the fact that the Magic only made two of their 16 three-point shots. Dennis Scott, who had returned from his injuries, missed an uncharacteristic six out of seven tries, and Scott Skiles threw up five bricks and only one successful three-pointer. But the Magic out-rebounded the Nets, 54 to 38, and New Jersey went down quietly.

Then, against Detroit, Shaquille made his first really serious mistake of the season. All season long, players throughout the NBA had been getting into ugly fights on the court, and now it was Shaquille's turn to lose his temper.

While Scott Skiles, Dennis Scott, and Nick Anderson were all busy scoring in the mid-20s, Shaquille had missed nine out of 11 shots, and only scored a very low total of seven points. With only 12 rebounds and no blocked shots, he was playing worse than he had all season. This overshadowed the fact that the Magic were beating the Pistons for the first time ever.

Deciding to take advantage of Shaquille's bad night, surly Pistons center Bill Laimbeer started fouling him late in the game, so that Shaquille would have to go to the line to try and make his shots. Shaquille took offense at this, and when he started yelling at Laimbeer, Detroit's Alvin Robertson tried to break up the potential struggle, so Shaquille hit *him* instead. He was immediately ejected from the game, and Robertson and Isiah Thomas were soon to follow.

The NBA management had grown very tired of players scuffling with one another, and Shaquille was fined $10,250, as well as being suspended for the Magic's next game — without pay. So, that one ill-advised punch cost Shaquille $46,835.

It was a mistake he didn't want to make again.

11
Another Shaq Backboard Craq

As it turned out, that immature punch also cost the Magic their next game, against the Charlotte Hornets. The game was played on April Fool's Day, and when viewers tuned in, it seems likely that most of them hoped that Shaquille's not being allowed to play was a joke. It wasn't. The Magic played hard, but Shaquille's backups, Greg Kite and Brian Williams, couldn't do anything to stop Charlotte center Alonzo Mourning, who dominated the game with 30 points. The Magic lost 102–93, and if they ended up missing the final playoff spot by one game, this loss to the Hornets would be one that everyone, especially Shaquille, would remember.

A week later, the Magic were able to get a little revenge when they met the Hornets again — this time, *with* Shaquille. Shaquille held his fellow rookie, Alonzo, to 21 points, while coming up with 29 himself, and the Magic won the game with no trouble.

The playoff race was still very close. The Magic remained a game and a half behind the Pacers, with only ten to play. They also had to watch out for the seasoned Detroit Pistons, who had been keeping pace with them all year long. Every game they played now was a big one.

First, the Magic met the Minnesota Timberwolves, and Christian Laettner, one of Shaquille's biggest rivals from their college days. The game was close all the way through, but as time was running out, Nick Anderson came up with the big basket when it counted, more than making up for an otherwise poor night from the field. Shaquille topped both teams in scoring, and rejected six of the Timberwolves' efforts, summoning that little bit of extra effort he always seemed to find when he went up against a Laettner or a Mourning.

Then, the next night, the Magic went down in defeat against the Milwaukee Bucks, negating one of Anthony Bowie's best performances all season, as he scored 20 points to match Shaquille's 20.

But the Magic didn't have time to worry about that loss, since they were scheduled to play the Bucks again just three days later, and they were able to salvage a split in the two-game series, winning 110–91. Dennis Scott was the hero this time, nailing nine three-pointers, for a total of 41 points. Since Indiana had lost to the Boston Celtics, the Magic, the Pacers, and the Pistons were now in a three-way tie for the last playoff slot.

With only seven games left in the season and their first playoff berth on the line, Shaquille and his teammates couldn't afford to let down at all. They went on the road to Philadelphia and Cleveland for two games — and promptly lost them both, slipping back behind Indiana and Detroit in the standings.

In Philadelphia, the 76ers not only double-teamed Shaquille, but they *triple*-teamed him. He still produced a team-high 21 points, but the Magic were blown out by a 101–85 score.

In Cleveland, after being down more than 20 points, Shaquille and his teammates came almost all the way back to win, before finally falling short, 113–110. Shaquille topped both teams in scoring and rebounds, but despite strong help from Dennis Scott and Donald Royal, the Magic just couldn't quite bring the game home.

Now, there were only five games to play, and the Magic needed every one of them. An inexperienced team will sometimes make the mistake of looking too far ahead, and not concentrating on the game in front of them, so Coach Guokas and his staff had to make sure to keep Shaquille and the rest of the team properly focused. The *next* game is always the only one that should matter.

In their final week, the Magic started off against the Celtics. Neither team looked very good, scoring a total of only 23 points in the fourth quarter, but the Magic lucked out with a victory. Shaquille, Dennis Scott, and Tom Tolbert were all handicapped by foul trouble, but since the Celtics seemed to be sleepwalking through the game, it didn't matter. Boston's front court stars Xavier McDaniel and Robert Parish only came up with 21 points and nine rebounds *between* them, which was a good indication of how poorly the Celtics really did play.

But good, bad, or ugly, a win was still a win, and the Magic put together a much prettier effort against the Washington Bullets two days later. Shaquille scored 20 points, and completely controlled the boards with 25 rebounds. This was his seventh 20–20 game of the season, a record of which a seasoned star would be proud, to say nothing of a barely twenty-one-year-old rookie.

With that win against the Bullets, the Magic were just a game behind the Pacers, who had lost to the Hawks that same evening. With three games to play, Shaquille could only hope that his team would keep winning, and the Pacers wouldn't.

Orlando was full of confidence when they flew up to Boston to meet the Celtics in the famous Boston Garden, where so many championships had been won and lost over the years. Having beaten Boston only a few days earlier, the Magic were ready to do it again.

Unfortunately, the Celtics had different ideas. Needing a win in order to guarantee having the home court advantage in the first playoff round, Boston — in NBA jargon — "came to play."

Guard Sherman Douglas paced the team with 11 assists and 24 points, while five other Celtics also scored in double figures. Shaquille and Scott Skiles both scored 20 points, but with Nick Anderson sidelined by hamstring problems, the team was missing the extra scoring punch they needed. When the final buzzer sounded, the Celtics had 126 points, and the Magic had only 98.

Orlando's playoff hopes were very slim now, especially since they were flying on to New Jersey to face Derrick Coleman and the always-tough Nets. Everyone's attention should have been solely on the outcome of the game, but when Shaquille went up for a routine dunk in the first quarter, he managed to break the unbreakable.

It is one thing to shatter a backboard. It is another thing to collapse the backboard support system, the way Shaquille had done in the game against Phoenix. It is still *another* thing to break the steel supports of a backboard in half. Basically, Shaquille tore the entire mechanism apart. More than a few observers wondered if it was even humanly possible to do such a thing. Surely, such a feat could only be accomplished by a Man of Steel. But the evidence was lying in a crumpled heap of metal on the floor.

Either way, this was no ordinary Shaq Attaq — it was absolute *Shaqnificence.*

Actually, Shaquille was very lucky not to have gotten hurt, since the entire backboard came down on top of him, and the cumbersome twenty-four-second shot clock glanced sharply off his head. But Shaquille just walked away as though it had been another dull day at the office. In the meantime, all of the players on the court joined the crowd in a standing ovation. Shaquille told the media that it hadn't hurt because he was a "knucklehead."

The damage to the backboard fixture was complete, and the game was delayed for over forty-five minutes while workers assembled a new backboard and shot clock. When Shaquille was coming to town, everyone knew to stock up on extra backboards. The broken shot clock added a new twist to the story.

The Nets had been ahead 25–21, but when the referees finally indicated that it was time to start playing again, Nick Anderson came into the game, ignoring his injured hamstring, and went on an offensive tear. In fact, Nick had his best game ever as a pro, scoring an awesome 50 points in only 33 minutes of playing time.

The Nets' bad luck continued. When Nets center Sam Bowie accidentally collided with Shaquille — with Shaquille's elbow, to be precise — he broke his nose and had to stop playing. Later on, Derrick Coleman ended up on the bench, too, after almost collapsing from exhaustion. Even so, the Nets were still clinging to a six-point lead with two minutes to go. But the Magic hung tough, and ground out a hard-earned 119–116 victory.

Now, there was just one game left to play, and

the only way the Magic could get into the playoffs was if they won, and the Pacers lost their game against the Miami Heat. The Magic were going against the Atlanta Hawks, in front of yet another capacity crowd at the Orlando Arena. With Shaquille on the team, the Magic had sold out every single home game during the 1992–1993 season.

Together, Shaquille and Nick Anderson teamed up to score almost 60 points, with Scott Skiles and Dennis Scott also reaching double figures. Shaquille also had 18 rebounds, while Scott Skiles kept the ball moving from his point guard position, garnering 14 assists. The Hawks, with the exception of flashy star Dominique Wilkins, floundered, after an initial flurry of scoring to start off the game. But late in the first quarter, the Magic took control and then cruised home with a 104–85 win.

This victory gave the Magic a final record of 41 wins and 41 losses for the season. That was twenty more games than they had won the year before, and everyone knew that Shaquille had made the difference. Now they just had to wait and see how the Pacers fared against the Heat.

But, to the team's disappointment, Indiana beat Miami, and qualified for that much-desired eighth playoff spot. This confused some people since the Magic and the Pacers had identical 41 and 41 records, but the NBA has established a very clear set of deciding factors in the event that two teams tie for the final spot.

The first tie-breaker is based on the results of

the two teams' games against each other during the season. Since Orlando won two of the four games they played against the Pacers, and lost the other two, on that criteria, they were still tied.

The second tie-breaker compares the two teams' records within their conference; in this case, the Eastern Conference. But, once again, Orlando and Indiana had won and lost the exact same number of games against Eastern teams, with records of 27 victories and 29 losses.

So, it was on to the third tie-breaker, which looks at the teams' records against the other teams that qualified for the playoffs in their conference. Improbable as it seems, Orlando and Indiana had posted the exact same record — again. They had each won 13 games, and lost 17, against other qualifiers.

When the NBA officials got to the next tie-breaker, they finally came up with a winner. The fourth tie-breaker adds up the numbers of points each team scored against the other team during the season, and sees who scored more. Since Indiana had scored 444 points in their four games, and the Magic had scored only 439, the tie was broken.

Indiana was in the playoffs, and Orlando was finished for the year.

Not everyone likes the tie-breaker system, and it does seem a little silly that a team can be out of the playoffs because of five points they did or did not score, in games that may have been played months earlier, but it is the fairest system that anyone has been able to devise so far. Truthfully, the situation doesn't come up very often, anyway, so sitting around and dissecting every point that was scored, or games that should have been won, and weren't, would be a waste of time. The important thing for Orlando to remember was that they had improved their record by twenty games, and that they had *almost* made the playoffs for the first time in franchise history. They had also won eight of their last twelve games, playing solid, winning basketball when it counted the most. They had every reason to be proud of their performances.

Next season, Shaquille and his teammates would just try to improve even more.

12
The Sky's the Limit

It would have been exciting to go to the playoffs, but Shaquille could look back on an absolutely unbelievable rookie season. He had not only helped his team to their best record in years, but he also ended up among the league leaders in almost every important statistical category. Shaquille had, every day, in every way, measured up to people's wildest expectations.

It comes as no surprise that Shaquille led the NBA in slam-dunks, with 270 thunderous jams. That works out to an average of more than three a game. While a few other players, like Golden State's Chris Mullin, shattered backboards during the eighty-two-game season, Shaquille was the only one who *destroyed* entire backboard units. Therefore, he was also the only player to accomplish that *twice*.

In total scoring, Shaquille ranked ninth in the NBA, with 1,862 points, and a 23.3 point-per-game average. That put him close behind the three other top centers in the game — Patrick Ewing, David Robinson, and Hakeem Olajuwon. Shaquille came in second in the NBA in rebounding, behind Dennis Rodman, with 1,104 rebounds and a 13.8 rebounds-per-game average. This made him the first rookie in over ten years to break the 1,000 mark in both scoring and rebounding. Shaquille was also second in the league in blocked shots, with a 3.56 average, for a total of 285 blocks. Only Hakeem Olajuwon placed ahead of him, with a mind-blowing 4.16 blocks-per-game average.

When all the numbers were added up, it turned out that Shaquille was the *only* player in the NBA to finish in the top ten in scoring, rebounding, blocked shots, *and* field goal percentage. With statistics like that, it wouldn't be long before he started bringing home the NBA's Most Valuable Player award. Being selected as the NBA's Rookie of the Year was, of course, a foregone conclusion, and Shaquille received 96 of the 98 votes, the other two going to Alonzo Mourning.

"Shaquille really is unique," *Orlando Sentinel* reporter Tim Povtak said recently. "And I think he's handled his celebrity status better than anyone expected. I know he's made my job easier."

Reebok representative Dave Fogelson feels the same way. "His impact has just exceeded everyone's expectations, both on and off the court," he said. "Obviously, along with everyone else in our business, we felt that Shaquille was going to be an impact player, but no one could have predicted the success that he's had this season. The statistics speak for themselves."

When asked for *his* opinion, Coach Dale Brown from LSU had a very simple answer. "He's become Mr. World," he said.

How did Shaquille measure up to the other premier centers in the NBA? Although the Magic split their four games with the Knicks, Shaquille matched Patrick Ewing almost every step of the way. Patrick usually edged Shaquille in the scoring contest, but Shaquille dominated the rebounding and blocked shot categories. When he played against David Robinson and the San Antonio Spurs, Shaquille had 19 points and 13 rebounds, to David's 23 points and 16 rebounds. So Shaquille came very close, but David's greater experience carried the day. In the next couple of years, David's advantage will probably disappear.

The only time Shaquille was really outplayed was by Hakeem Olajuwon. In their two games, Shaquille outrebounded Hakeem, but Hakeem scored 42 points and blocked nine shots, while Shaquille scored only 28 and blocked five. Derrick Coleman also gave Shaquille a little trouble here and there, but the only other player in the NBA who really caused him any difficulties was Dennis Rodman. Since Dennis may be the best defensive player in the league, it isn't surprising that Shaquille had a few problems against him.

Every team in the NBA had learned that the only possible way to stop Shaquille was to cover him with at least two defenders, and sometimes three. Even that wasn't always enough, but it was the best they could do.

It is worth mentioning that Shaquille was also doing good and interesting things off the court. While his rap-singing with the Fu-Schnickens and his appearance in the movie *CB-4* may have gained the most publicity, Shaquille spent time helping people who are less fortunate than he is, too.

"Shaquille has done a number of things to help the Orlando community, like feeding hungry people during Thanksgiving," Reebok representative Dave Fogelson revealed. "He also gave toys away to children at Christmastime."

Shaquille not only donated money to feed the homeless, but he even worked on the serving line during the meal. Throughout the Christmas season, he put on a red stocking cap, and personally handed out his gifts to needy children.

"Shaquille also pays for a couple of dozen kids from the Orlando area to come to every Magic home game," Dave Fogelson said, describing the "Shaq Paq" program, which awarded tickets to students in exchange for their attending school regularly. "And we help with that," Dave went on, "making sure that the kids walk away with a Shaq Reebok T-shirt when they go to those games. Like our other contracted NBA players,

Shaquille will also be involved with our court renewal program, where we go and refurbish outdoor basketball courts. Reebok wants to work closely with him on projects that are of interest to him."

One of Shaquille's other endorsement companies, Spalding, also has plans to take advantage of Shaquille's desire to help others.

"We're putting together a 1-800 phone line where kids can call in and hear Shaquille being interviewed," spokesperson Scott Dickey said. "They can hear him talking about what it's like to be in the NBA, and what it was like playing basketball in high school and college. He'll also be talking about staying in school, and staying off drugs, working hard to do the right things, listening to your parents — things like that. One of the most important factors we considered in getting involved with Shaquille is what kind of role model he is, and what his values are like. The way his parents brought him up, and the values that have been instilled in him, make him a natural tie-in for a company like us."

Shaquille has always enjoyed being around children, and there is general agreement that he *is* an ideal role model, who stays away from so many of the temptations that have plagued other young celebrities.

"Even given his size, younger people don't feel threatened by him at all," Dave Fogelson said. "They feel very comfortable with him."

"He's at his best around the kids, because I

think he's still a kid himself," reporter Tim Povtak agreed. "He's a businessman, he's a millionaire, and yet I think the times that he enjoys the most are when he does any of the promotions with the kids. It looks to me like he *beams*. This year, there was a halftime promotion where these little six-year-olds were dribbling a basketball and racing upcourt, but they all had to wear Shaq's size 20, triple E shoes. He just howled when he saw that. I mean, he thought that was the funniest thing, watching these little six-year-olds trying to stomp up and down the court in his size 20 shoes. I really think he's happiest when he can be around kids."

But even though Shaquille was only twenty-one and still sometimes felt like a kid, he had never once played like one. The big question now is how good can he become? He is already one of the best players in the NBA, if not the entire world, and is it even possible for him to take his game to a higher level? Could *anyone*?

His defense, rebounding, and shot-blocking are all uniformly excellent but, as described earlier in this book, Shaquille does have skills he can improve. He will probably work the hardest on practicing his free-throw shooting, but he can also expand some other aspects of his offense. He needs a dependable move to the basket that doesn't emphasize his power, but rather his skill. Developing a little touch shot, like Patrick Ewing's short hook, would broaden his game immeasurably. He could also work on a skyhook.

Shaquille can also work on improving his jump shot. When a player can drop back ten or fifteen feet from the basket and sink that shot consistently, his overall scoring potential is multiplied. Even the *threat* of an excellent jump shot is enough to make defenders wary, and gives a center more freedom to score from the low post position.

Coach Brown agrees with the general evaluation of Shaquille's abilities. "He *is* only twenty-one, so he has a long way to go," he said. "He's an inferior free-throw shooter, so he needs to accomplish that, and he needs to work on his hook a little more."

With more experience, Shaquille will also be able to get rid of the ball faster when he is double-teamed. Passing is a skill that doesn't get mentioned very often, but a team that can't move the ball well is a team that won't succeed. The part that finesse plays in a center's arsenal is what separates the Hall of Famers from the merely *good* athletes. Developing game savvy and overall finesse can take years of practice, but Shaquille is certainly well on his way.

"This is a guy who came into the NBA last year weighing 300 pounds," *San Antonio Express News* reporter Dave Flores said, when he was assessing Shaquille's future. "Wilt Chamberlain only — I say 'only' — came in at 275, Patrick Ewing was a lot slimmer when he came into the league, and certainly Bill Walton was. Never has there been a guy with Shaquille's physical attributes. Just four short years ago when he was at Cole High School, he was already doing a lot of what he's doing now, and you could tell that he was going to be something special. I mean, you just *knew* it, because the guy was so strong."

"He has the *potential* to be the greatest player in the history of the league," Orlando reporter Tim Povtak agreed. "In any *sport*, in the history of sports. He may never get any better than he is now, but even if he doesn't, that's still pretty good. It's his first year, and he's already an All-Star. If he has the right mental makeup, who knows? No one his size has ever been that athletic, and when you put those two things together — the sky's the limit."

Dave Flores also had some thoughts about the less obvious intangible gifts that Shaquille has. "What's always impressed me about him is that he has a lot of heart," Dave said. "You could say that he has to polish his game, and develop a shot, and everything else, but I didn't have any doubt that he would do well. He's the kind of guy who just loves to compete. He has pride in himself, and in his game, and he's definitely not going to back down from anybody. A lot of other players don't have that edge. The thing about Shaquille is that he's always going to *play*. He is certainly unique."

It is safe to say that Shaquille already has all of the physical tools — and more — that he'll need to break every record in the book. His biggest challenge will be trying to cope with the mental aspects of the game, and not getting burned out from the pressure of other people's expectations. The glare of publicity, the lure of the limelight, and the long grueling days and nights of the eighty-two-game seasons can take their toll.

Shaquille will also have to work hard to create the proper balance between his natural desire to lead a normal life, and the demands that super-stardom imposes. Maybe the hardest thing of all will be reminding himself to have *fun*, when the whole world seems to be watching every move he makes.

But, after just one season, using his unique combination of talent and charisma, Shaquille has helped lift the NBA to new heights of popu-larity. Basketball fans all over the world will be looking forward to seeing him accomplish even bigger and better things in the years to come.

For Shaquille, the sky really *is* the limit.

Awards and Honors

High School

- Led Cole High School to a 68–1 win-loss record over two years
- Helped team win the Class 3A Texas State Championship his senior year, with a 36–0 record.
- Player of the Year, Greater San Antonio, senior year
- Class 3A All-State Team, Texas, senior year
- Most Valuable Player, Dapper Dan Classic game
- Most Valuable Player, McDonald's All-Star Classic game
- Selected to the *Parade* magazine All-America team, 1989

College

- Two-time consensus pick, first team, All-America, 1991–92
- Two-time consensus pick, Southeastern Conference (SEC) Player of the Year, 1991–92 (first LSU player ever to win this award)
- The Associated Press's Rupp Award (for the National Player of the Year, college basketball), 1991
- National Player of the Year, UPI, 1991
- *Sports Illustrated* National Player of the Year, 1991
- Tanqueray World Amateur Athlete of the Year, 1991
- National Player of the Year, L.A. Gear, 1992
- Runner-up, Naismith Award (to Christian Laettner), 1992
- Runner-up, John Wooden Award (to Christian Laettner), 1992
- Southeastern Conference (SEC) All-Defensive team, Most Valuable Player, 1991–92
- SEC all-time leader, blocked shots (412)
- Most blocked shots, three consecutive years, SEC
- First player to lead SEC in rebounding, three years running, since Charles Barkley
- Ranked first in the nation, college level, blocked shots, 1991
- Ranked first in the nation, college level, rebounding, 1991
- Ranked second nationally, rebounding, 1992

- First player ever to lead SEC in rebounding, scoring, field goal percentage, and blocked shots in the same season, 1991
- SEC leader in rebounding, field goal percentage, blocked shots, 1992
- Ranked seventh, all-time, SEC, rebounding
- Ranked second, all-time, SEC, career field goal percentage
- First LSU player to have back-to-back 400-plus rebounding seasons, 1991–92
- Ranked second, all-time, LSU, career rebounding
- Ranked third, all-time, LSU, career scoring
- Ranked second, all-time, LSU, career field goal percentage
- Six career triple-doubles at LSU (double figures in rebounds, points, and blocked shots in a single game)

Professional Basketball Career

- First player selected overall, NBA draft, 1992
- NBA Rookie of the Year, receiving 96 out of possible 98 votes
- First rookie ever to be named NBA Player of the Week during first week as a professional player
- NBA Rookie of the Month, four months in a row
- First rookie since 1985 (Michael Jordan) to be voted to the starting lineup, NBA All-Star Game
- Youngest athlete ever to play in an NBA All-Star game

- Led Orlando Magic to most victories (41) in team franchise history
- Only player in NBA ranked in the top ten in scoring, rebounding, field goal percentage, *and* blocked shots, 1992–93 season
- Led NBA in slam-dunks (270)
- Second in the NBA, rebounding, 1992–93 season
- Second in the NBA, blocked shots, 1992–93 season
- Ninth in the NBA, total scoring, 1992–93 season
- First rookie in over ten years to break the 1,000 mark in both points scored and rebounds
- Produced 68 double-doubles, rookie season

Career Statistics

High School

Scored 522 total points, junior year

Year	G	RPG	BLK	PPG	PTS
1988–89	36	22.0	8.0	32.1	1,123

College

Year	G	FG/FGA	PCT.	FT/FTA	PCT.	PTS	PPG
1989–90	32	180/314	.573	85/153	.556	445	13.9
1990–91	28	312/497	.628	150/235	.638	774	27.6
1991–92	30	294/478	.615	134/254	.528	722	24.1
Totals	90	786/1289	.610	369/642	.575	1,941	21.6

Year	REB	RPG	AST	STL	TO	BLK
1989–90	385	12.0	61	38	93	115
1990–91	411	14.7	45	41	99	140
1991–92	421	14.0	46	29	103	157
Totals	1,217	13.5	152	108	295	412

NBA

Year	G	FG/FGA	PCT.	FT/FTA	PCT.	PTS	PPG
1992–93	81	721/1288	.560	420/710	.592	1,893	23.4

Year	REB	RPG	AST	STL	TO	BLK	BLK AVG
1992–93	1,122	13.9	149	59	300	285	3.53

Guide to Abbreviations:

G = Games
FG/FGA = Field goals/Field goals attempted
PCT. = Percentage
FT/FTA = Free throws/Free throw attempts
PTS = Points
PPG = Points per game
REB = Rebounds
RPG = Rebounds per game
AST = Assists
STL = Steals
TO = Turnovers
BLK = Blocked shots
BLK AVG = Blocked shots average, per game

SCHOLASTIC BIOGRAPHY

About the Author

Ellen Emerson White is the author of several Scholastic Biographies, including *Jennifer Capriati, Bo Jackson: Playing the Games*, and *Jim Abbott: Against All Odds*. She is also an acclaimed writer of fiction. Her many books include *Life Without Friends* and *Long Live the Queen*, an ALA Best Book for Young Adults.

Ellen Emerson White lives and writes in New York City.